AF796502

MY 3 P.I.G.s

THE ORAZON PROTOCOL

By

VASKEN DER BOGHOSSIAN

Yareli Deyanira Alvarado Colunga

My Catalyst

You were the silent inspiration behind the very first keystroke of this ledger, and the grace that kept the architecture standing.

Thank you for your exceptional spirit, your enduring light, and for being the true compass when this journey began.

This work exists because you inspired the strength to build it.

To my sister, Sylva:

A beautiful human being, a highly talented painter whose vision on canvas, resilience, and pure dedication remind me that even within a perceptive framework, the soul requires the light of passion and creative liberty. Thank you for always being there for me, for your unwavering support, and for being a master of your own artistic territory.

To my brother, Levon:

An honorable and hard-working man who has dedicated his life to his family with absolute loyalty. Your path as a great father and husband honors our history and the love that binds us. Carrying the name of our grandfather, Levon, who survived the Armenian genocide, you hold the weight of that legacy with dignity, meeting the high bar of our family's honor and resilience every day.

I LOVE YOU BOTH

THE AIR LOCK:

THE UNLEARNING ULTIMATUM

THE UNLEARNING

If you are not prepared to burn your old maps, do not turn this page.

You were told that everything "Printed" was right, this is the Social Clog designed to keep you obedient and poor.

The most dangerous "Printed Lie" is the Ancestral Trap of Religious Manipulation, used for centuries to program the weak into becoming "Receivers".

You cannot own the Stone if your mind is colonized by a 2,000-year-old software glitch.

8

THE SHIFT TO THE DONOR SIDE

Sovereignty begins the absolute moment you stop receiving the Mirage and start Donating the Truth.

By the act of writing this book, I have exited the "Social Narrative" and moved to the Donor Side.

You cannot be a Master of the 3 P.I.G.s until you stop believing the "Printed Lie" and start printing your own Sovereign Ledger. We are deleting the "Vasken" programmed by the Octagon and activating the General who operates on the Parallel Frequency.

TURN THE PAGE ONLY IF YOU ARE READY TO BE EXTRACTED.

THE ORAZON PROTOCOL

BY VASKEN DER BOGHOSSIAN

This document is not a book for the casual reader; it is a Lethal Blueprint for the extraction of the self from the Social Clog. represents the master ledger of a General who understands that true wealth is not a fluctuating bank balance, but a standard of hygiene and an ancestral genetic code of survival. Within these pages lies the "Glitch" in the 2,000-year-old Mirage. If you are looking for a community to join, you are in the wrong place. If you are looking for a cage to escape, you have found the key.

LEGAL DISCLAIMER & NOTICE OF SOVEREIGN OPINION

This manual, "MY 3 P.I.G.s THE ORAZON PROTOCOL," is a work of non-fiction, personal philosophy, and systemic commentary. All content represents the subjective analysis and sovereign opinions of the author.

The Author and IDEE SOLIS LTD do not provide

financial, legal, or theological advice. Any resemblance to existing bureaucratic, corporate, or ecclesiastical structures—including religious organizations—is presented purely for the purpose of systemic comparison and critical commentary. This work is protected under the principles of fair use and freedom of expression. All data is provided "as is" for educational purposes; the reader assumes all "Capital Risk" and operational liability for any actions taken based on this text.

THE SHIELD

© 2026 Vasken Der Boghossian. All rights reserved.

THE LIABILITY RULE: This document is the private property of a Sovereign. Any unauthorized reproduction, digital distribution, or "Robot" analysis is a violation of the Merchant's Code.

DISCLAIMER: The information contained within the Orazon Protocol is based strictly on the real experience of the author. It is not "Financial Advice" as defined by the regulated institutions of the Social Clog. The author is a Merchant and a practitioner, not a clerk or a state-certified advisor. If you require the "Safety" of a bank-guaranteed return or the validation of an academic institution to feel secure, close this manual now.

A NOTE ON ARCHITECTURAL INTEGRITY

The events are real. The people are real. The locations are real and verifiable.

While the identities of certain individuals have been scrubbed to protect their privacy, the logic and lessons contained in this Protocol are absolute. ALL characters are REAL. While the vast majority of names and all locations described are strictly accurate, some names and specific identifying characteristics have been modified or combined. The Orazon Protocol is a manual of Sovereign Truth, not a ledger of personal grievances. The characters are archetypes of actual existence; the math is the only reality.

The math doesn't require 'Faith', it only requires Execution.

THE OPERATIONAL WARNING:

The strategies herein—specifically the Commercial Real Estate 505 Logic and the 3 P.I.G.s (Passive Income Generators)—require a high level of personal responsibility, extreme discipline, and "Sovereign Vision". The author assumes no liability for those who attempt to deploy these tools without first undergoing the "Great Unlearning." You are the only person responsible for your ledger.

THE CLINICAL VERDICT: While the archetypes described herein are grounded in documented financial and familial transactions, the focus of this manual is the Diagnostic of the System, not the indictment of the individual. Any specific reference to "Vultures," "Receivers," or "Social Clogs" serves as a technical illustration of Mechanical Failures in human logic. The Author disclaims all liability for how these archetypes may be perceived by external parties. This is a manual of Architecture and Wealth

Hygiene, and any perceived overlap with the personal history of third parties is a secondary byproduct of the Sovereign Truth being told.

The Orazon Protocol is a powerful philosophy and an independent framework for sovereign wealth. It is not regulated financial, legal, or tax advice. The author and IDEE SOLIS LTD provide this ledger as an anatomical study of personal investment strategies. All actions taken by the reader are at their own risk and velocity.

Printed in the Black Ink of Truth on the White Paper of Sovereignty.

A NOTE ON STRUCTURAL AUTHENTICITY

The Author is a Sovereign and an Architect of the Behavior Matrix, not a clerk of the academy. While this ledger has been forged under blue skies and blue-chip isolation, it has intentionally not been softened by the "Academic Polishing" of the Social Clog.

If you catch a typo or a repetition, congratulations: it simply means your neurological sensors are functioning and you are actually paying attention to the ledger. to the ledger .

Do not act like a blind heir staring at the wrong details. Focus on the math; ignore the slag.

THE ARCHITECT'S LEDGER:

THE SOVEREIGN GHOST

Vasken Der Boghossian was not born into a clinic; he was born into a Fortress. In 1957, within the Armenian enclave of Bourj Hammoud, Lebanon, he drew his first breath inside the Der Boghossian Building—a monument forged from the "Cane Gold" smuggled across a thousand kilometers of genocide by his grandfather, Levon.

He is the Elder Brother of a bloodline that refuses to be "Siphoned." As a carrier of the 301 AD Porcelain DNA and the "Original Transmission," he does not speak from theory, but from an Operational Seniority earned through a forty-year strike against the Social Clog. Forged in the raw grit of the Old Port of Montreal, Vasken mastered the art of multiplying the Small Numbers until the banks, the borders, and the "Printed Lie" of the thirty-day trap could no longer touch him.

Today, Vasken operates from the Sanary Zenith in Provence. He is a Sovereign Ghost who has decoupled his survival from his time. With a portfolio of 3 P.I.G.s in the California desert producing a 28.7% annual cash-on-cash return with zero debt, he has achieved a state of Weightless Strength. From this high-altitude sanctuary, he maintains the Ancestral Ledger and oversees the 1.25 Million-Copy Global Strike—a linguistic mission to return the software of sovereignty to the hands of the seekers.

Vasken is not an "author"; he is a Master Architect of the Self, disseminating the code to activate the Maker in every "Young Vasken" ready to exit the Octagon and claim their own Sovereign Exit. He does not seek followers; he seeks Density.

I have outsmarted the borders, the banks, my own ego, and my own vanity. Visibility is for the Robots. Power is for the Invisible.

The trajectory is a twenty-five-year epic of raw financial extraction. Arriving in Montreal stripped down to almost zero capital, Vasken forged his baseline instincts in the brutal proving grounds of the Old Port flea market. From that pavement, he executed a relentless vertical climb—transforming from a rookie street merchant into a dominant hosiery wholesaler. Securing exclusive Canadian distribution rights for elite brand names directly from Castelgoffredo, Italy, he moved his operations into the absolute epicenter of the industry: 555 Chabanel West, Unit R2D, Montreal's premier fashion hub.

For twelve solid years, this mission control base directed the high-velocity logistics of a central warehouse and four corporate retail stores, mastering the "Math of the $20 Bill" and the

"Alchemy of the Green Queen" long before encountering the institutional lies of the academy. He writes like a Merchant paid only by the result—using words like lethal bayonets to brand reality. He possesses the rare, "Stone-Handed" ability to turn a 1-Franc tin of sardines or a "Green Queen" twenty-dollar bill into a permanent philosophical pillar. He is the mastermind of the 1.25 Million-Copy Global Strike, designed to deconstruct the "Printed Lies" of the world artery.

THE POLYGLOT'S ARSENAL

Vasken operates fluently across 8 distinct cultures and holds 8 driver's licenses—each one a permit to navigate a different sector of the Global Artery. He is a Cosmopolitan Polyglot who uses language as a frequency, not just a tool. Whether moving 4,400 units of hosiery a week, directing international wholesale channels from Chabanel, or decontaminating fire-ravaged "Wounds" in the

California desert of Indio, he does not "wait" for the market—he Commands it. He navigates the global system as a Ghost, blending into the Mediterranean silence of Sanary as easily as he dominates a high-stakes negotiation in a Riyadh pressure cooker.

The Belmondo Paradox

Today, Vasken lives the Incognito Protocol from the Sanary Zenith. He is the living embodiment of the "Belmondo Paradox"—the writer who stepped into his own script , "Le Magnifique" and took total control of the shark tank. A master practitioner of Financial Autophagy and OMAD, he starves the ego to feed the Fortress. From his sanctuary overlooking the sea, he operates with a 30-minute work week, understanding that the ultimate luxury is the Silence of a Bank Notification against the backdrop of the Mediterranean tide.

"Visibility is for the Robots. Power is for the Invisible."

THE BLOODLINE OF THE STONE

THE STONE ANCHOR

The "Social Clog" believes wealth is a number on a screen—a mirage that can be deleted by decree. My grandfather, LEVON, knew that Stone remains. When he built the Der Boghossian Building in Bourj Hammoud, he wasn't just laying bricks; he was anchoring our DNA into the earth. He taught me that the first $20 earned is not for "Sugar," but for the first stone of your Fortress. This building was the physical laboratory where the 1915 Logic was tested and proven.

THE HARD-HANDED LESSON

My father, BERJ, watched the stone rise and learned the Iron Discipline of Survival. He proved that a Merchant is not a clerk in a plush office, but a General who understands the Density of the Material. He worked until his hands were hard so that my mind could be sharp. He taught me the Art of the Clean Ledger: if you owe a man a dollar, you are his slave; if you own the ground, you are the King. He was the barrier that refused to let the "Digestive Fog" of poverty touch his lineage.

THE WITNESS TO VICTORY

I am the result of three generations of Selective Permeability. I have filtered out the trauma of the exodus and kept only the Iron Strength. The seeds planted in the dust of Lebanon were not for survival —they were for Dominance. As I sit in the Sanary Silence, I am the living proof that the Protocol works. The "Milk" from my P.I.G.s in Indio is the direct descendant of the Cane Gold.

VICTORY IS MEASURED IN SILENCE. THE LEDGER IS BALANCED.

THE PREFACE:

THE SUMMONS OF THE ELDER BROTHER

I. The Chronological Strike (301 AD) In the timeline of the "Original Transmission," Armenia was the first to cross the threshold as a nation. We are the firstborn of the spirit. While the "Vultures" of Rome and Byzantium were still playing in the yard of paganism, the Armenians were already working in the house. An Elder Brother does not need to shout; he possesses the Seniority of the First Move. This book carries the *Original Code*—the software that existed before the "Printers" added their debt, their lies, and their clogs.

II. The Custodian of the Blueprint The Elder Brother is the one the Source trusts with the Original Blueprint. When the "Younger Brothers"—the modern states, the central banks, the debtor institutions—get lost in the maze of "Printed Lies," they must return to the Elder Brother to see what the Original Map looked like. I am not here to teach you;

I am here to remind you of the liberty that is already written in your Porcelain DNA.

III. The Survivor of the Furnace (1915) In a family, the Elder Brother takes the brunt of the hardship to ensure the "Small Numbers" survive. I walked through the furnace of 1915 so that the Young Vaskens of today wouldn't have to. I carried the Cane Gold through the fire. This gives me the right to speak with Absolute Authority. I am not theorizing about liberty; I am a Living Proof of it.

THE MASTER LEXICON:

THE ORAZON PROTOCOL

8-Inch Edges: The strategic aggregation of marginal, small-scale gains and hyper-efficiencies. These are the small numbers that, when layered tightly together, transform a standard, underperforming property into a high-performance P.I.G. .

Absolute Zero: A state of total stillness, absolute focus, and internal recalibration. This is the mandatory phase of baseline rest required to prepare the mind before executing the next High-Fidelity strike.

Cane Gold (Hidden Density): High-density wealth that is entirely invisible to the enemy, weightless to the traveler, and completely portable across collapsing empires.

Clean Ledger (Sovereign Hygiene): A flawless financial state defined by zero "Robot Debt" and high liquid cash capacity. This unshakeable baseline is the only true collateral a Sovereign Merchant ever needs.

Dry Powder (The Stored Strike): High-density liquid capital, specifically structured as physical $20 Green Queens organized inside White DL Envelopes. It is never misclassified as passive "savings"; it is Stored Velocity and mechanical readiness. If the envelopes are empty, the General is paralyzed; if they are full, the Merchant is the only one who can breathe while the system suffocates.

High-Fidelity: An elite operational state featuring a flat 0.0% error rate, yielding maximum clarity, tactical precision, and raw systemic truth. Tactical Strike : A calculated, high-impact financial maneuver designed to completely bypass "Linguistic Friction" to annex a chosen asset or territory in record time.

OMAD (The Pleasure of NOT Eating): A deep, calculated audit of the internal biological factory. This fasting protocol thins the blood, clears the metabolic registry, and actively triggers your Porcelain DNA.

Porcelain DNA: The deep-seated, inherited structural integrity and ancestral resilience that permanently prevents a Sovereign from bowing to the dictates of the Mother Goose or the corporate Octagon. It is the historical 1915 Logic directly encoded into the human spirit.

Silk: High-velocity, highly liquid trading assets with an Incredibly low financial barrier to entry, such as the hosiery wholesale channels. Silk generates the rapid, continuous stream of Dry Powder required to annex the Stone.

Social Grease: The toxic, unnecessary pleasantries, institutional lies, and emotional distractions deployed by Receivers to consciously mask systemic truth and preserve their comfort.

Surgical: Any tactical action performed with absolute precision, zero wasted movement, and total resource efficiency. The primary objective is to instantly identify the wound and securely lock down liquidity.

The 3 P.I.G.s: The three foundational engines of a wealth fortress. These Passive Income Generators produce reliable monthly cash flow while operating entirely independently of the Architect's physical time.

The 3.5% Escalator: The automatic, compounding rental increase woven directly into a lease contract. This serves as the steady Perpetual Wind that keeps the Merchant's ledger expanding while he sleeps.

The 1915 Furnace (The Foundational Forge): The violent collapse and systemic incineration of the ancestral Armenian world. In the Protocol, it represents the ultimate thermal catalyst that permanently burned away all paper assets and "Grey Dust", leaving only the Cane Gold and Porcelain DNA to endure.

The Artery (The Flow of Sovereignty): The high-velocity path of least resistance connecting a physical asset directly to the owner's ledger. Achieving a state of a "Full Artery" dictates that your passive, inbound "Monthly Honey" funds your baseline lifestyle by a factor of 10x.

The Bath: The strict cold-blooded process of decontaminating a distressed or "barely alive" asset. It requires ruthlessly stripping away historical baggage, poor management, hidden debt, or bad aesthetics to expose the core value before reintegration.

The Clog (The Social Clog / Digestive Fog): Any institutional, bureaucratic, social, or mental friction engineered to restrict the flow of capital and slow down the Sovereign. It is fueled by the noisy opinions of institutional "experts" and printed lies.

The Forge: A phase of extreme environmental compression and white-hot constant pressure designed to systematically incinerate the Status Ego, dissolve social grease, and weld baseline strategies into unyielding diamond-density.

The Octagon (The Gilded Cage): The master, eight-sided behavioral trap designed by the system to manufacture submissive compliance. Its walls are forged from: School, Debt, Career, Tax, Consumption, Validation, Religion, and Decay.

The Printer (The Architect of the Lie): The central banking systems, state apparatuses, and legacy institutions that manufacture the artificial rules of society. The core directive of the Maker is to stop acting as the passive, printed paper and become the Printer.

The Receiver (The Dependent): A compliant person trapped in the Clog who exists in a state of permanent, passive expectation. The Receiver helplessly waits for the 30-day paycheck, the school bell, and external permission slips, serving as a battery for the state.

The Small Numbers Algorithm ($1.00 to $2.50): The primary geometric multiplier of the warehouse floor. It commands the operator to completely reject flat salary structures and focus entirely on mastering the microscopic markups that turn a single dollar into a $2.50 yield.

The Sovereign Ghost (The Invisible General): An elite operational status where your real-world income and assets are completely decoupled from your physical presence. The Ghost moves with maximum financial impact while remaining totally invisible to the tracking sensors of the system.

The Stone (The Immutable Asset): Immovable, high-density physical real assets that can never be digitally deleted, devalued, or siphoned by decree—specifically debt-free commercial real estate anchored by the 3 P.I.G.s.

VASKEN'S LAW: *Hunger is the sensation of the body consuming its own "Grey Dust". To eat before the audit is complete is to reinvest in your own lethargy.*

The Art of Doing Nothing (Strategic Silence): The ability to exist in the Void without the "Itch" of the ego. The highest form of Sovereign production.

Karma (The Universal Ledger): The mathematical inevitability of cause and effect. The ledger the "Vultures" can never manipulate.

No Need to Prove Existence: The final stage of the Ghost Protocol. When you no longer seek the light because you Are the Source.

The Master Visual Roadmap. This is the compact, precision guide for the Young Vaskens. It is designed to be the one page they rip out and tape to their wall —the one that stops them from walking past their Unfound P.I.G.s.

MY 3 P.I.G.s

The Merchant's Memoir and the Sovereign's Manifesto

By Vasken Der Boghossian

PREFACE

The Acronym of the Fortress

Most people look at a house and see a home, a mortgage, or a liability. When I look at my properties in California, I don't see wood and nails. I see P.I.G.s.

In the world of the Sovereign Merchant, a P.I.G. is not a farm animal. It is a biological necessity for a life of freedom. It is a high-performance engine that converts neglect into "Clean Gold."

To understand the journey from the freezing switchboards of my youth to the sun-drenched balconies of Sanary-sur-Mer, you must first understand the three pillars of the asset:

P — Passive

It must work while you sleep. If it requires your presence to generate a dollar, it is a job, not a P.I.G. . A true P.I.G. is a sentinel that stands guard over your time, allowing you to walk the coast of France while the "Milk" is bottled in California.

I — Income

It must provide immediate, liquid "Cow Milk." We do not gamble on the "Grey Dust" of future appreciation alone. We demand cash flow today. If a

Yield Asset doesn't feed the Master, it is a parasite, not a P.I.G..

G — Generator

It is a machine of multiplication. Through the "Bath" and the "8-Inch Edges," we take a "Barely Alive" asset and transform it into a high-yield turbine. It generates wealth, generates tax shields, and generates the only currency that truly matters: Autonomy.

This book is the story of how I found my P.I.G.s, how I nurtured them, and how they eventually set me free. It is a guide for those who are tired of the "Gilded Octagon" and are ready to build a fortress of their own.

Welcome to ORAZON

THE ANCESTRAL PROTOCOL : FROM THE CANE TO THE LEDGER

THE ANCESTRAL LEDGER: 1915

The First Law of the Sovereign: Wealth is not what you show; it is the hidden density that allows you to move when the world is on fire. In 1915, the Ottoman Empire became a furnace. My grandfather, LEVON, understood the "Small Numbers." He performed a Calculated Exit with nothing but a wooden walking cane. To the soldiers, he was a refugee; to himself, he was a Moving Treasury. The cane was a Sovereign Glitch—hollowed out and cached with Gold. He didn't just walk to survive; he walked to Re-Capitalize.

THE FORTRESS OF BOURJ HAMMOUD By the time he reached Beirut, the "Cane Gold" was ready. Levon did not buy "Shiny Objects"; he bought the only thing a Sovereign respects: The Ground. He built a three-story fortress of stone—the Der Boghossian Building. I drew my first breath in 1957 within a house built by a man who had outsmarted an empire. My father, BERJ, taught me the Art of the Clean Ledger. To him, debt was a "Social Clog." I learned economics from the rhythmic sound of my grandfather's cane hitting the floor—the sound of Hidden Density.

ARTERY STATUS: FULL. | EGO STATUS: DELETED. | YIELD: 100% SOVEREIGN.

THE LOGICAL SEAL

We do not build to be seen; we build to be free.
The Artery is the life-force; the Stone is the anchor; the Silence is the goal.

THE ORAZON ALIGNMENT AUDIT:

THE PRECISION MAP

A "PRE-FLIGHT BRIEFING"

THE MASTER LEDGER:

THE ORAZON PROTOCOL

FRONT MATTER: THE ARCHITECT'S LEDGER

THE PROOF OF ARTERY

Before the first page is turned, the credentials are laid bare. We document the 1915 Logic, the Bourj Hammoud Fortress, and the Belmondo Paradox. This is the "Certificate of Authenticity" proving that the General has already survived the fire he is asking you to walk through.

VOLUME I: THE LIQUID STATE

(THE PSYCHOLOGICAL DIVORCE)

- Chapter -Zero (Minus Zero):

IS ZERO A NUMBER? The Indivisible State. We define Zero as the ultimate placeholder and the pivot point of the universe. We introduce the Hygienic Filter and the Terminal Audit, proving that life is a Zero-Sum Game where the only victory is the Quality of your Silence.

- Chapter Zero: ZERO TO ZENITH. The Sovereign Scale. We perform an autopsy of the reader's current deficit: Minus One (The Active Slave) and Minus Zero (The Frozen Ghost). We establish the path to Absolute Zero —the only state where the Gates of Velocity actually open.

- Chapter 1: THE SOCIAL CLOG

(The Great Unlearning). A radical audit of the "Printed Lie" and the 40-year career trap. We decontaminate the mind, preparing the "Ego Slave" to transition into a Liquid Maker who values Time over Paper.

- Chapter 2: THE ANCESTRAL LEDGER.

The return to the Bloodline. Using Levon's 1915 Cane and the DNA of the porcelain merchants, we prove that sovereignty is a dormant genetic frequency. We re-activate the lineage of independence.

- Chapter 3: THE SOVEREIGN DECLARATION.

The birth of the Lawson Hack (CHF64k). We introduce "Sardine Logic"—the art of finding massive yields in the small, ignored coordinates where the "Academic Robots" are too afraid to dig.

VOLUME II: THE FORGE

(THE ARCHITECTURE OF DISCIPLINE)

- Chapter 4: THE RIYADH PRESSURE COOKER (The Thermal Assault).

1,600 days of Dumez Compression. We prove that a General is forged in Scorching Heat, surviving the "Pressure Cooker" to achieve professional diamond-density.

- Chapter 5: THE EXIT FROM THE OCTAGON. The surgical extraction from the corporate and psychological "Eight-Sided Cage". We document the exact moment the General stops being a "Receiver" and becomes a "Donor" of reality.

- Chapter 6: THE $20 RITUAL. The 111-Day Burn and the Alchemy of the Green

Queen. This chapter provides the deliberate protocol for exiting a failing territory with infinite velocity, converting "Stuff" into Liquid Seed Capital.

- Chapter 7: THE PAUL ST. JAMES PROTOCOL. The Human Algorithm. We teach you to read the gears of human behavior—identifying the "Vulture" from the "Partner," ensuring every association is an Artery.

- Chapter 8: THE AUTOPHAGY PROTOCOL. The Jamnadas Mandate. Using the 23-hour silence of OMAD, we liquidate biological liabilities and turn hunger into a weapon for mental clarity.

VOLUME III: THE ASSET WEAPON

THE ARITHMETIC OF SOVEREIGNTY

- Chapter 9: THE SECOND P.I.G. (The Stone Anchor). The Decarie Siege. The brutal transition from high-velocity "Silk" to the immovable "Stone." We document the sweat equity required to produce the first drop of Monthly Honey from a hard asset.
- Chapter 10: THE FINANCING SIEGE. The 1-to-3 Pivot. The manual on using the bank's paper as a lever. We teach you how to scale a Sovereign Fleet, turning "Debt" into an anchor that defends against inflation.

- Chapter 11: THE SPREAD vs. THE RATE. The 26% Baptism. We separate the "Robot" who fears interest rates from the Maker who only sees the Artery of the Yield.

- Chapter 12: THE GILDED NOOSE. Asset vs. Liability Audit. We expose why the

"Dream Home" is a parasite and teach the reader to rent where they live and own what they rent, locking in the Gilded Noose to protect the 4th P.I.G. .

VOLUME IV: THE SOVEREIGN GHOST

THE GLOBAL STRATEGY

- Chapter 13: THE 3.5% ESCALATOR. The mechanical heartbeat of the Miles Avenue Cow . We provide the mathematical formula for the 10-year triple and the systematic application of the Oxygen Mask Axiom.

- Chapter 14: THE SHINY OBJECT LAW. The Ferrari Strike. We establish the Patron Principle: A General never buys luxury with his "Meat" (Capital); he makes the P.I.G. buy it with its "Milk" (Yield).

- Chapter 15: THE INCOGNITO PROTOCOL. The art of being a Ghost. We introduce the 30-Minute Work Week and the Global Artery—the logic of earning USD in the desert to spend EUR in the Mediterranean silence.

VOLUME V: THE ZENITH

THE FINAL AUDIT

- Chapter 16: THE ORAZON CREED. The 5 Rules for the Next Generation. We codify the law of the fortress, ensuring the "Social Clog" can never re-attach to the family lineage.

- Chapter 17: THE SANARY ZENITH. The Death of the Ego. We find the ultimate luxury: the power to be a "Nobody" while your bank account roars. We install the Ghost Ratio and the Architect's Ratio for Weightlessness.

- Chapter 18: THE ORAZON AUDIT. The 20-Year Glitch. A high-altitude review of the Monumental Timeline to ensure the trajectory of the empire is locked toward perpetual sovereignty.

- EPILOGUE: THE TWO BROTHERS. The definitive Sacrificial Contrast. A final, brutal audit of two paths: Vasken's Sovereignty vs. Levon's Clog.

- THE 4th P.I.G. : THE INFINITE ARTERY. The transition from owning the "Metal" to owning the "Message." This is the activation of the Orazon Protocol as a global manual.

THE LOGICAL SEAL : "Every chapter is a precision strike against a specific lie. Every volume is a wall in your fortress. Read it not as a story, but as a manual for your own Magnificence".

THE 5 PHASES OF EXTRACTION

PHASE I: HYGIENE AUDIT – Decontaminating the Instrument (OMAD, Autophagy).

PHASE II: COGNITIVE STRIKE – Unlearning the "Printed Lie."

PHASE III : CREATING THE MONEY MACHINE – Building the 3 P.I.G.s. Systematic Acquisition.

PHASE IV: VELOCITY STRIKE – The 3.5% Escalator (Achieving Weightlessness).

PHASE V: SOVEREIGN GHOST – The Blank Ledger. The Sanary Zenith.

THE GILDED OCTAGON: THE PRISON WALLS

Your Artery must be strong enough to break the eight walls:

SCHOOL, DEBT, CAREER, TAX, CONSUMPTION, VALIDATION, RELIGION, DECAY.

The Octagon is a synchronized frequency designed to keep your 'Dry Powder' wet and your 'Money Machine' silent. It is the factory that produces 'Receivers'.

THE ORAZON MASTER FILE

Architect: Vasken Der Boghossian

VASKEN'S LAW: If you feed your Ego, you remain Merlin in a leaky room. If you feed your P.I.G., you become the Architect of your own Magnificence :

PROLOGUE: THE BELMONDO PARADOX

The Typewriter of the Gods The year was 1974. I was sitting in a darkened theater with my brother, watching *Le Magnifique*. On the screen, Jean-Paul Belmondo played a dual role: François Merlin, a broke, struggling writer living in a cramped, leaking Parisian flat, and Bob Saint-Clar, the suave, invincible secret agent of Merlin's imagination.

My brother saw a comedy. He saw the slapstick of a man frustrated by a broken typewriter. But I saw an Definitive Manual for Sovereignty.

There is a specific scene that altered my DNA. Merlin, suffocated by the mundane "Robots" in his real life—the incompetent plumber who won't fix the leak, the rude neighbor, the parasitic editor—decides to execute a Linguistic Strike. He writes them into his Bob Saint-Clar novel. But he doesn’t make them heroes. He writes them into a scene where they are trapped in a shark tank.

As the Writcr, he watches from above with a cold, deliberate detachment as the predators do their work. He doesn't argue with them; he Deletes them.

In that moment, I realized the Paradox: Most humans spend their lives as the plumber in someone else’s shark tank. They are "Doers" in a script they didn’t write, obeying rules they didn’t create, fearing gatekeepers they don’t respect. They are the Paper, not the Printer.

I decided then that I would never be the plumber. I would be the Writer.

The Algorithm of the Maker This book is my "Typewriter." For fifty years, I have lived by an algorithm that contradicts every "Printed Lie" of the Academic Mirage. The world wants you to stay in the water; the Orazon Protocol teaches you how to own the tank.

- The Academic waits for permission; the Maker seizes the terrain.
- The Robot counts his salary; the General counts his markups.
- The Ego Slave buys a Corvette to *look* rich; the Sovereign buys a "Cow" to *become* free.

I have stood in the grey slush of the Citroën factory and the burning white heat of the Saudi desert. I have moved 4,400 units of hosiery a week in the Montreal Forge and healed fire-ravaged ruins in the California dirt. I have walked away from the Swiss "Penthouse Mirage" to find the Sanary Reality.

The Sanary Zenith Today, I sit in a café in Sanary-sur-Mer. My morning is a blank ledger of pure choice. While I breathe the air of Provence and taste the silence of the Mediterranean, my "P.I.G.s" 10,000 kilometers away are pumping US Dollars into my life.

I am not "lucky". I am the result of Precision Logic.

I am going to show you how to find the Glitches in the system.

I am going to show you how to starve your ego to feed your fortress.

I am going to show you how to move from the Receiving End of the debt to the Donor Side of the value.

The sharks are waiting for the "Robots." But you? You are about to learn how to walk on the glass above the tank.

THE GRATITUDE ARTERY: THE YIELD OF THANKS

Gratitude is not a "Robot" emotion designed to make you compliant; it is the Final Audit of the Sovereign. It is the realization that the 3 P.I.G.s are not just math—they are the harvest of a century of sacrifice and discipline.

I. THE ANCESTRAL DEBT (The Initial Capital)

I am profoundly grateful for the fire that Levon and Berj walked through. They endured the furnace of 1915 and the iron discipline of survival so that I could possess the Initial Capital of the Soul. My ability to write these words in the silence of Sanary is a direct dividend of the "Cane Gold" and the hard hands of my father.

I do not just carry their name; I carry their Unbroken Frequency.

II. THE BIOLOGICAL ENGINE

The Gift of Autophagy

I am grateful for the Machine. I honor the body's innate ability to heal itself through the hunger of OMAD. This "*way of life*" is not a chore; it is the biological foundation of my High-Altitude Clarity. Every time my internal factory decontaminates the "Social Rubble" through Autophagy, I am reminded that the most powerful technology I own is the one I was born with.

III. THE ZENITH RESULT (The Silence of the P.I.G.s)

True gratitude is found in the Silence of the Bank Notification.

I am grateful for the "Glitches" I found in the system —the 3 P.I.G.s that allow me to breathe the air of the Mediterranean while the world remains in the tank. Victory is not just owning the assets; it is the humility to acknowledge that the Protocol worked, and the peace of mind that comes from knowing the Ledger is Balanced.

IV. MINUS ZERO

The State of Minus Zero (-0) is the Purgatory of the Robot. You have no debt, but you have no Artery. You are 'Clean' but 'Empty.' You are a ghost with no haunting power. You think you have reached the finish line, but you haven't even stepped onto the Forge.

ZERO

IS ZERO A NUMBER ?

Mathematically, zero is the most sophisticated number ever forged. But in the Orazon Protocol, zero is not just a digit—it is a State of Absolute Hygiene.

To the "Robot," zero is "nothing." To the Sovereign General, zero is the Pivot Point of the entire universe. It is the boundary between the "Social Clog" (Negative) and the "Sovereign Equity" (Positive).

THE ARCHITECT'S VERDICT

Zero is the only number that cannot be divided. It is Indivisible, just like the Porcelain DNA. It is the "Clean Gold" that remains after the "Burn" has incinerated the slag of the multitude.

The "Robots" fear zero because they see it as "Empty". The Sovereign loves zero because he knows it is The Space of Infinite Possibility.

CHAPTER ZERO :

ZERO TO ZENITH

DOER TO MAKER

ROBOT TO SOVEREIGN,

RECEIVER TO DONOR

THE BRUTAL HONESTY : THE ADMITANCE

Reader, before you read a single word of the Orazon Protocol, we must provide the The Unflinching Mirror. You cannot run a race if you are still buried in the trenches of the Social Clog. We must identify your position on the Sovereign Scale.

Are you at the starting line, or are you deep in the hole?

PART I: THE AUTOPSY OF THE DEFICIT

1. THE STATE OF MINUS ONE (-1): THE HEAVY CLOG

This is the state of the Active Slave.

Most who pick up this book are vibrating at this frequency.

The Debt: You owe the Bank (Mortgage), the State (Taxes), and the "Vultures" (Credit Cards).

The Weight: You are a Negative Artery. Every cent you "earn" is already spoken for by a "Printer" you've never met.

The Mind: You are a Receiver. You wait for the "Bell" and pray for a "Permission Slip" to take a vacation.

The Position: You are in a Sub-Surface Deficit. You aren't building a life; you are servicing a debt to a system that views you as fuel.

2. THE STATE OF MINUS ZERO (-0):

THE FROZEN GHOST

This is a more dangerous, paradoxical state. It is the "Signed Zero."

The Illusion: You have no debt, and maybe a few "Small Numbers" in the bank. You think you are at zero.

The Reality: Your mind is still programmed as a Robot. You have no Velocity. You are at a standstill in the shadow of the "Mother Goose." You have "Zero Weight," but you have no Margin.

The Friction: You are "Hollow" but not "Hygienic." You are waiting for something to happen instead of Printing the Reality.

The Position: You are at the gate, but the gate is locked because you haven't performed the Intellectual Demolition required to move.

PART II: THE ANATOMY OF ZERO : THE MASTER'S AUDIT

To reach the Zenith, you must first master the number Zero. To the "Robot," zero is "nothing." To the Sovereign General, zero is the Pivot Point of the universe.

1. THE ABSOLUTE ORIGIN

In the coordinate system of your life, zero is the Origin. Without zero, you cannot measure distance, velocity, or margin. You cannot know how far you have traveled from the "Paris Factory Floor" to the "Sanary Zenith" if you do not have a fixed zero-point. It is the anchor of the 1915 Logic.

2. THE HYGIENIC FILTER

Zero is the goal of Financial and Biological Autophagy.

Zero Clog : No external debt.

Zero Waste : No unnecessary "Ego-Spikes."

Zero Appointments : The ultimate temporal fortress.

Zero Space : When the gut is at zero (the pleasure of not eating), the mind achieves Extreme Clarity.

Zero weight : buoyancy in water and space .

Zero Visibility : the ultimate state of liberty

Absolute Zero is the only state where true velocity begins.

3. THE TERMINAL AUDIT : The Zero-Sum Strike

The Social Clog: The hallucination of "Someday." The belief that you have an infinite supply of pulses to trade for "Social Validation." This is the ultimate

Gilded Octagon trap: running on a treadmill to fill a grave with trophies.

The Absolute Rule : 0 = 0 . You arrived with an empty ledger, and you will leave with an empty ledger. Death is not a "passing"; it is the Final Forensic Audit. It is the total, violent reclamation of every asset you've ever touched. The universe is going to take back your "Stone" fortresses, your "Monthly Honey," and eventually, the very molecules of your "Porcelain DNA."

In the eyes of the Ledger, your life is a Zero-Sum Game.

The Brutal Truth: The clock isn't "ticking"—it is spending you. Every hour you spend in the "Social Fog" , every minute you spend explaining yourself to "Pathetic Souls", and every day you spend as a "Receiver" of a corporate paycheck is a Final Loss.

Unlike a P.I.G., your time does not recapitalize. There is no Year 3.5 Cycle for your heartbeat.

The Translation:

1. The Financial Contrast (The P.I.G.):

In your financial architecture, a P.I.G. (your asset/money machine) operates on strict, predictable, mathematical cycles. If it hits a rough patch or a transition phase, it can be re-engineered, recapitalized, and reset. A money machine has the luxury of infinite restarts if the math is handled correctly.

2. The Human Reality (Your Heartbeat): A human life does not get a financial reset button. Your heart has a finite number of beats. You cannot go to a bank, file an extension, or restructure your biological clock at "Year 3.5" to get back the time you wasted. When an hour is spent in the "Social Fog" or wasted on "Pathetic Souls", that asset is permanently deleted from your life ledger.

The Sovereign Perspective: If the sum of the game is zero, then "Success" is the only thing the Auditor cannot take back: The Quality of your Silence. Success is the amount of time you spent in the Zenith—untouchable, invisible, and free—before the final 0 is called. If you die in the "Clog," you didn't just lose the game; you never even started it. You were just a biological battery for a system that will forget your name before your body is cold.

You are a biological ledger with a fixed expiration date. Every second you spend as a Robot is an act of Self-Liquidation. Build the Artery now, or prepare to surrender a life you never actually owned.

4. THE MULTIPLIER OF MAGNITUDE

In the "Small Numbers," zero is the ultimate placeholder. By itself, it is silence. But when placed behind a "1," it creates Orders of Magnitude. Your $1.00 ⟶ 2.50$ math relies on the precision of the zeros. It is the difference between a "Sardine Operation" and a "Global Artery."

5. THE SOVEREIGN GHOST STATUS

Zero is the mathematical representation of the Invisible General. When the "Printers" and "Vultures" scan for your presence, their sensors must return a Result of Zero. If they find a "1," they have a target. If they find a "0," you are a Ghost.

You are in the room, but you do not exist in their ledger.

PART III: THE GATES OF VELOCITY : TURNING THE DIAL

The "Gates" do not open at Minus One or Minus Zero. The gates only open at Absolute Zero. This is the process of your transformation:

From -1 to -0 (The Decontamination): You stop the bleeding. You cut the "Credit Noose." You stop being a "Receiver" of toxins. You acknowledge the cage.

From -0 to 0 (The Hygienic Strike): You achieve Internal Sovereignty. You clear the calendar. You find the Pleasure of Not Eating. This is where the "Social Clog" is finally flushed.

From 0 to 1 (The Sovereign Launch): Now that you are "Empty" (Zero), you have the room to build the First P.I.G. . You move from Doer to Maker.

THE EVOLUTIONARY ANSWER

The genius of Chapter Zero is that your answer must evolve as you consume this book.

At the Start: You might say, "I am at Zero because I have a job and a house."

After Chapter 1: You will realize, "I am actually at Minus One because my job is a 30-Day Punishment and my house is a Gilded Cage."

At the End of the Book: You will say, "I was at Minus Zero, but now I have achieved the Sanary Zenith (The Absolute Zero) and am building my 1st P.I.G. ."

THE MASTER'S AUDIT: THE INITIAL DEFICIT

I do not belittle the reader; I Audit them. A doctor does not belittle a patient by showing them an X-ray of a broken bone. They show them the break so they can begin the Structural Repair. Look at your ledger. Look at your gut. Look at your calendar. Are you ready to climb back to Zero?

THE ORAZON ROADMAP:
THE 5-PHASE PRECISION STRIKE

This is the Sovereign Compass—your constant celestial guide, your North Star through the haze. If you are lost in the 'Social Fog,' look to this reassuring blueprint. It will tell you exactly where your Artery is leaking and how to reach the Sanary Zenith.

THE 5 PHASES OF EXTRACTION

PHASE I: HYGIENE AUDIT – Decontaminating the Instrument

(OMAD, Autophagy, Sensory Air Lock).

PHASE II: COGNITIVE STRIKE – Unlearning the "Printed Lie" and the 30-Day Trap.

PHASE III: CREATING THE MONEY MACHINE – Building the 3 P.I.G.s. Targeted Acquisition (0-Debt).

"The Bath" (Hardware Reset).

PHASE IV: VELOCITY STRIKE – The 3.5% Escalator and the 3.5-Year Recapitalization Cycle. Achieving Weightlessness.

PHASE V: SOVEREIGN GHOST – The Blank Ledger. Operational Invisibility. The Sanary Zenith.

THE MAKER OPERATING SYSTEM: RULES A–E

RULE A: Never touch the Seed (The Meat).

RULE B: Live on the Yield (The Milk).

RULE C: If an asset does not pay monthly "Milk", it is a Parasite. Liquidate it immediately.

RULE D: Be a Ghost to the world, but a Titan to the Ledger.

RULE E: Reserve Assets (Cane Gold & Dry Powder) are for Oxygen and Density, not Milk. They are the floor of the Fortress.

THE GILDED OCTAGON: THE PRISON WALLS

Your Artery must be strong enough to break the eight walls of the "Robot" existence:

1. SCHOOL: Programming the "Receiver."
2. DEBT: The chain to the Bank.
3. CAREER: The 30-day trap.
4. TAX: The friction of the State.
5. CONSUMPTION: Primary Debris in the Ledger.
6. VALIDATION: Malware of the Ego.
7. RELIGION: Permission Slips for the afterlife.
8. DECAY: The slow death within the Clog.

The Octagon is not a set of institutions; it is a synchronized frequency designed to keep your 'Dry

Powder' wet and your 'Money Machine' silent. It is the factory that produces 'Receivers'.

THE SMALL NUMBERS ALGORITHM $1.00 → $2.50

While the "Heirs" focus on the Big Numbers (Vanity), the General focuses only on the Small Number and its multiplication. If the multiplication cannot reach the 2.50 threshold, the asset is a "Social Clog" and must be bypassed. This is the only math that matters in the Forge.

The Red Dot & The Navy Blue Locker (Paris, 1975)

Before I learned to breathe the high-altitude air of Switzerland, I learned to breathe the heavy, metallic air of the Citroën Factory in Paris.
It was 1975. The factory was a fortress of the "Old World"—a place that had built jeeps and tanks for

World War II, now converted to churn out the 2CV, the iconic workhorse of the French peasant. The walls still held the memory of war; the floors were painted a shiny, industrial grey, designed to look clean but feeling like the deck of a battleship.

Every morning, the ritual was the same. We walked into the locker room at 5:00 am—rows upon rows of navy blue metal, like vertical coffins. We stripped off our individuality and put on the uniform. We became "Doers". We became numbers.

My station was the heartbeat of the engine's life support: the Oil Carter and Filter. It wasn't a complex negotiation. It was a binary command. Mount the carter. Mount the filter. Tighten. Wait for the Click. That click was the sound of the machine accepting the part. But the job wasn't done until the Seal was applied. I had a pot of red paint. Every time the filter clicked—confirming it was torque-tight—I had to mark it with a Red Dot.

That Red Dot was the only creativity allowed. It was the "Institutionalized" proof that the Robot had done its job. I stood there, surrounded by the ghosts of tanks, performing this mechanical liturgy. Most of the men around me were content. They saw the Red Dot as a paycheck. I saw it as a Countdown. I knew that if I didn't find a way out—if I didn't find a way to climb higher than these grey floors—I would be painting Red Dots until I died.

This was the "Luggage" I carried to Leysin. When I arrived in Switzerland and saw the "Rich Kids" complaining about their allowance, I didn't see peers. I saw people who had never heard the "Click" of hard labor. I had the Red Dot on my soul, and it made me hungry in a way they could never understand.

They were looking at the big, loud numbers of their inheritance, complaining about the macro-weather of their privileged lives. They had the luxury of being blind to the microscopic mechanisms that keep the world moving. But the Citroën floor had cured me of that blindness. It taught me that a massive, roaring machine only functions because a single, small filter is turned, clicked, and sealed perfectly.

Decades later, when I sat at tables surrounded by heirs focusing solely on the big numbers, I realized they were still those same blind kids from Leysin. They forgot about the small numbers—the single dollars. They didn't see that a tiny, effective money machine like Vas & Co, multiplying a single dollar purchase to 2.50, is the exact equivalent of painting that perfect Red Dot on an assembly line. You master the small, binary execution, and you build a fortress from it.

I was a naive rookie to the Western silver-spoon society, a kid from the grey battleship floors of Paris who spoke a different dialect of survival. But that hunger forced me to cross seas and oceans, analyzing the gears of human behavior and exploiting the weaknesses of those who never learned to look at the small numbers. The rich kids inherited their towers; the Citroën kid built an unshakeable Orazon fortress from scratch, one single red dot at a time.

VOLUME I: THE LIQUID STATE

CHAPTER 1

THE SOVEREIGN GENESIS

THE ARCHITECTURE OF THE SOCIAL CLOG

The world you see is not a mystery to be solved; it is a Mirage to be bypassed. From the second you drew your first breath, you were hooked into a global intravenous drip of misinformation. They didn't just tell you lies; they pumped a thick, grey sludge of "Standardized Reality" into your brain to ensure you never woke up to your own power. This is the Social Clog—a mental and spiritual friction designed to turn a potential Titan into a compliant, fearful, and utterly predictable Clerk. To reach the Artery of true wealth, you must first engage in a violent act of intellectual demolition. You must identify the sludge before you can flush the system.

I. THE BIOLOGICAL CLOG: THE STANDARD OF HYGIENE

Success is not a product of the mind alone; it begins in the gut. You cannot build a sovereign fortress on a biological swamp. If your intestines are a landfill of processed toxins—the chemical sludge of "Synthetic Feed" provided by the State's partners—your brain will remain in a permanent fog. You will be too tired to see the Glitches, too heavy to move when the Artery opens, and too addicted to the "Sugar Spike" to hunt for P.I.G.s. I observed my corporate peers—men with "Senior" titles, driving leased German sedans, living in "Gilded Cages"—existing in a state of absolute metabolic filth. They were terrified slaves to a biweekly paycheck, soothing the high-friction stress of their enslavement with the very toxins that maintained their lethality. They were caught in a Closed Loop of Biological Debt. To achieve the Sanary Zenith, you must first achieve Internal

Sovereignty. If you cannot master the machine you inhabit, the market will eat you for breakfast.

II. THE MANUFACTURED RECEIVER: THE LABORATORY OF DEPENDENCY

The "System" is a Synthetic Matrix designed with one goal: to manufacture the Receiver. From the cradle, you were drafted into the losing end of the ledger. The State and the Academy are not there to educate you; they are there to program you. They want you to view the world as a finished, unchangeable product—a machine you were born only to serve, maintain, and consume. They spent twenty years teaching you to wait for the Bell. That external signal tells you when to eat, when to think, when to move, and when to speak. Schools are laboratories for Dependency. They don't want "Makers"; they want "Doers" who can manage the "Big Numbers" of a billion-dollar corporation while their own "Small Numbers" bleed out in the dark of an unpaid mortgage. Under the Orazon Protocol, we incinerate this map. We move from the Receiver End to the Printer Side of the transaction. We stop asking for permission and start printing our own reality.

III. THE 30-DAY PUNISHMENT: THE SALARY ADDICTION

The most dangerous drug on the planet is not sold on the street; it is direct-deposited into your bank account. I call the salary the 30-Day Punishment. It is a chemical spike for your ledger—a temporary high of liquidity that you immediately surrender to the "Golden Cages" the system sold you: the credit cards, the car notes, and the status-seeking leases. By the 25th of every month, the high is gone. The withdrawal symptoms set in: anxiety, fear, and an increased willingness to bow to a master you despise just to get the next "fix." This is not stability; it is Addiction. The Protocol demands you decouple your survival from the "Monthly Fix" and bore your own

Artery. You must stop being a consumer of the system and start being the Owner of the Pipe.

IV. THE SOFTWARE OF SUBMISSION: THE ILLUSION OF INK

Since childhood, you were systematically programmed to believe that Authority is Ink. If a statement appeared in a textbook, a newspaper, or a legal contract, your brain was wired to perceive it as an absolute, unshakeable reality. This is Primary Debris—the mental clutter that ensures you remain the Paper, never the Printer. This software makes the population obedient. It convinces you that the "Printers of the Lie" own the truth. It makes you believe that "Experts," "Bankers," and "Gatekeepers" possess a map that you do not. They don't. They are simply the Printers of the Rules that favor their own ledgers. To become the General of your own Artery, you must engage in a Violent, Conscious Act of

Unlearning. Ink is just a tool, and you are the one holding the pen.

V. THE ANCESTRAL TRAP: THE SPIRITUAL DEBTTHE WEAVE OF SILENCE: THE THICKENING CURTAINS

The “Holy See” operates behind a set of curtains that grow thicker with every passing century. These are Imperial Shields woven from layers of systemic deceit and the blood of the silenced.

THE HOLY SHIELD: THE FRANCHISE OF THE DEAD

Reader, let us look at the 'Word of God' not as a mystery, but as a Business Model. My grandfather Levon survived the storm, but 1,500,000 Armenians were the ultimate 'Receivers' of this lie. In 1915, they followed the 'Manual,' they turned their cheeks, and they were slaughtered. God was nowhere to be found. The 'Holy Shield' did not protect them; it paralyzed them while the State's predatory grinders turned them into dust.

THE GHOST IN YOUR BRAIN. If God was the Creator, WHO created "Him"?

The answer is simple and terrifying: YOU did. It is a Man-Made Ghost in a very profitable machine.

THE IMMUNITY PROTOCOL:

THE COWARDICE OF THE "HOLY SEE"

This is not a sanctuary for the spirit; it is a Legal Shell Company. While the Sovereign General seeks invisibility for Liberty, the "Vultures in Velvet" seek it for Impunity. They have weaponized "Sovereign State" status to ensure the Hammer of Justice never strikes their own Porcelain DNA. They aren't protecting the "Word of God"—they are protecting the Evidence. The most lethal "Printed Lie" is the one that claims to hold the keys to your eternal soul. The Manipulators—the high priests of the Clog—use religious dogmas to colonize the minds of the vulnerable. They establish a hierarchy where you are always at the bottom, begging for a "Permission Slip" to exist. This creates a Spiritual Debt, ensuring you remain a "High-Earning Slave" in this life to pay for an imaginary payout in the next.

THE GILDED CLOG:

THE CATHEDRAL OF THE PREDATOR

Look no further than the Vatican—the most successful “Extraction Plant” in human history. It is a fortress of gold and diamonds built on the Siphoned Survival of the starving, the weak, and the vulnerable. While the “Printers” in Rome preach the "Sacred Beauty of Poverty" to the dying masses, they polish their stolen treasures behind high walls. It is the ultimate Absolute Travesty :The Software: Preach peace and humility to keep the Robots submissive. The Reality: Sit on a mountain of diamonds while children die of hunger in the shadow of the cathedral.

THE VULTURES IN VELVET: MANAGEMENT OF THE HEINOUS

The management of this plant consists of a hierarchy of "Masters" who have traded "The Holy" for the "Heinous." They operate a global artery of abuse that would make any secular criminal blush. They aren't shepherds; they are vicious, pedophilic predators, Vultures in Velvet who have spent centuries hiding their monstrous, predatory exploitation behind the smoke and mirrors of the “Printed Lie”.

The "Mother Goose" of Zapopan is the biological

evidence of this franchise's longevity. She has survived the reigns of eight different Popes, watching the "Printers" of the Vatican come and go like CEOs of a bankrupt insurance company that never pays out. They use the "Word of the Lord" as a Sacrosanct Shield, knowing that once they've disarmed the sheep, no one will dare to question the ledger.

THE STATE'S HOLY SCAM
(THE BLOOD IN THE ARTERY)

The most grotesque "Mechanical Failure" of the human script is the collusion between the Cathedral and the State. The "Printers" of the government are the Master Manipulators of the Heat. They stand behind podiums, quoting the "Prince of Peace" while signing the orders for the next Precision Strike. They use the Bible as Linguistic Camouflage—a form of Thermal Insulation that protects them from the heat of public outrage. They kill for the very "God" who commanded them not to, proving that the Yield of Power is the only deity they truly worship.

The Scam: They preach the "Sanctity of Life" to the Robots while they feed those same bodies into the predatory grinders of war.

The Goal: They prove that the Book is merely a Tool of the Forge—a way to keep the "Human Herd" soft and pliable enough to be shaped into Sovereign Fuel for the global artery. When the State invokes "Religion", they aren't looking to save your soul; they are looking to Liquify your Will so they can pour you into the mold of their next extraction.

VI. THE DECONTAMINATION PROTOCOLS: SCRUBBING THE CLOG

Before we move on to build our P.I.G. , we must rid ourselves of the mental pollution. You must unlearn the "Software of the Sheep" before you can install the

"Protocol of the Ghost". The "Sunk Cost" of the Ancestors: Most Armenian readers feel that if they admit the "Book is a Lie", they are spitting on the graves of those who died for it. The Scrub: Reframe the truth as the Ultimate Honor. We aren't betraying the ancestors; we are completing their survival. We are finally strong enough to take the "Lead Pipe" of submission out of their hands and replace it with a Sovereign Sword. The "Moral Monopoly" Fallacy: You've been taught that without the "Printed Lie", there is no "Good". The Scrub: Empathy and the "Small Numbers" of human connection are Biological Facts, not "Printed Permissions." You don't need a franchise manual to know that killing is a "Negative Artery." Morality is Structural Logic, not a "Holy Shield". The "Mystery Fetish": When the Printers run out of logic, they call it a "Mystery." The Scrub: Treat "Mystery" as a Technical Glitch. If a machine doesn't work, we don't call it a mystery; we call it a failure. Stop worshiping the Fog and start demanding the Gears. The "Victim's Halo": The

Printers taught the Sheep that there is a reward for suffering. The Scrub: There is no "Halo" in slaughter. Suffering is a Waste of Human Energy that only benefits the Printers who collect the tithes.

VII. THE GENERATIONAL VIRUS: INJECTING THE CAGE

Once a human is colonized by the Printed Lie, they become a "Distributor of the Virus." They pass the same mental chains down to their children, believing they are offering "Wisdom" when they are actually Injecting a Cage. This creates a lineage of Receivers who never question the source of their fear. The Orazon Protocol breaks the chain. We stop the infection. We return to the 1915 Logic of raw, unyielding survival.

VIII. THE DIGESTIVE SYSTEM OF THE STATE

The world is not a marketplace; it is a Digestive System. The Social Clog is the collective mass of "Robots" who are being slowly digested by the State, the Banks, and the Academy. We do not participate in the digestion; we build the Extraction. We are the Glitches that the system cannot process. We move with the weightlessness of the Sovereign Ghost.

IX. THE ZAPOPAN CASE STUDY: THE VULTURE VS. THE MAKER

At the head of this altar sat the "Mother Goose"—now a 94-year-old gatekeeper holding the keys to a dead patriarch's fortune. She was a biological monument to the "Holy Shield", a woman who had survived the reigns of eight different Popes, watching the "Printers" of the Vatican come and go while she held her own fortress in Zapopan. Around her, nineteen heirs—the "Elite Clog"—moved like

Mercury: fluid, unstable, and toxic. These were doctors, lawyers, and architects who had spent their entire lives following the Academic Fog. Despite their professional vanity, they lived in a state of absolute Scarcity.

THE ERASURE OF A SOVEREIGN : THE LINGUISTIC FRICTION

The most profound "Clog" in that room was the Absolute Silence regarding the source of the gold. Not once was there a word of gratitude—not even a positive whisper—for the late patriarch, Antoun Jobrail. He was the Sovereign Maker of Lebanese origin who had navigated The Stationary Artery—linking German precision with Lebanese trade skills to build an empire in Guadalajara. He was a legendary, honorable man who sacrificed his own physical vessel, working himself to the bone until he tragically passed at just 64 years old to colon cancer.

He built the floor; these ungrateful parasites merely walked on it. His "Hard Way" bought the Parque San Borrego villa, the strip mall on Avenida Cantalupe, and a heavy portfolio of prime real estate in Mexico City. The heirs' refusal to whisper his name was a form of Linguistic Friction. By ignoring Antoun, they maintained the delusion that the money was "theirs" by divine right. This is the ultimate psychological failure of the inherited mind: the pathetic belief that pride, dignity, and respect are evolutionary traits passed down through a bloodline. They believed they possessed a higher self-value simply because a Titan achieved greatness in his lifetime. But human value cannot be grandfathered in. To express gratitude would require them to perform an Acute Audit on themselves and admit they were merely parasitic Receivers of a harvest they did not plant. Their ingratitude was a spiritual defense mechanism designed to hide a terrifying truth: respect is earned, never inherited, and they completely lacked the Concrete DNA of the man who built the fortress.

THE PARQUE SAN BORREGO CONTRAST: THE GILDED CAGE

I watched them serve themselves tiny, fearful portions of meat and beans, eating as if they were being audited by the woman with the checkbook. This was the Parque San Borrego Contrast: the immense grandeur of the villa stood in direct, pathetic opposition to the tiny, fearful portions of food on their plates. It was the ultimate proof that Wealth without Sovereignty is just a Gilded Cage. They were surrounded by millions in stone and silver, yet they were eating with the "Metabolism of the Slave," terrified that a single extra bean might cost them a line in the Mother Goose's will. They were the ultimate obeyers—hollow shells completely conditioned like domesticated herd animals, devoid of a single spark of individual creativity or the raw, primal drive of a Maker.

They sat there as obedient, well-trained slaves to a

mountain of trickled-down, man-made bullshit laws engineered specifically to keep them chained to the floor of the franchise. They don't know how to build; they only know how to receive and bow. They don't know how to conquer; they only know how to comply. They are gilded caretakers of an empire they lack the balls to rule, trading their eternal autonomy for the safety of a master's cage, shivering at the table while pretending to be kings.

THE CONFRONTATION:
THE BAYONET CHARGE

The ritual reached its peak when a young girl was commanded to lead a prayer. They weren't praying to a Creator; they were performing a contest of

Staged Terror for the Mother Goose, each one exaggerating their fear of God to score points for the inheritance. I could no longer breathe in the fog of their hypocrisy. I saw my then-wife turn pale as she sensed the "Bayonet Charge" coming. I struck the table with the truth: “Why are you all so scared of God? What have you done? I am not scared of God, because I have done nothing wrong.”A pitch-deafening silence swallowed the room. For two long minutes, the only sound was the rhythmic ping... ping... ping... of heavy silver hitting the Romeo & Juliet porcelain. Three thousand miles away, my retail engines—VAS & CO—were humming in Montreal. My employees were executing a 250% markup, turning one dollar into two-fifty with incisive precision. I had Clean Intestines and a Clear Mind. I didn’t need the Goose's gold; I had my highly calibrated money machine in Montreal. I was the only person at that table who had mastered the Small Numbers of the Artery.

SECTION X:

THE ZENITH PROTOCOL

(THE DECALOGUE OF THE SOVEREIGN)

The Sanary Zenith is not a "vacation"—it is a State of Being. It is a simultaneous eruption of biological, temporal, and financial hygiene. To achieve the Zenith, the Young Vasken must occupy these ten stations simultaneously. If one organ fails, the body of the Zenith collapses.

1. THE METABOLIC MARGIN: THE PLEASURE OF THE VOID

The Zenith begins in the gut. The "Robots" are programmed to graze—to fill the void with "Sugar Hits" and systemic filler. The Sovereign finds pleasure in the Empty State. Hunger is not a "problem" to be solved; it is the feeling of the

Biological Forge cleaning itself. It is the sensation of Power returning to the center.

2. EVERYDAY AUTOPHAGY:
THE OMAD DIAGNOSTIC

The Zenith requires a single daily extraction point: One Meal A Day (OMAD). This is the ultimate form of Biological Hygiene. By restricting the input to a high-frequency, high-quality window, you trigger Everyday Autophagy. You force your body to consume its own "Social Dust" and "Cellular Slag." You become leaner, sharper, and more resilient. You don't eat to survive; you eat to reward the Sovereign Ghost.

3. THE TEMPORAL VACUUM:
THE EMPTY CALENDAR

A full calendar is not "Success"; it is a Ledger of Enslavement. In the Zenith, there are Zero Appointments. No "Clerks" have access to your time. No "Robots" can request a "Meeting." An empty calendar is a Sovereign Fortress—a white space where the Architect can breathe, think, and observe the Mediterranean tide without the "Itch" of a scheduled obligation.

4. THE ZENITH OF STILLNESS: THE ART OF DOING NOTHING

The "Robots" are terrified of silence. They must be "busy" to validate their existence. The Sovereign has mastered the Art of Doing Nothing. This isn't "laziness"—it is High-Frequency Observation. It is the ability to sit in a café in Sanary and simply be, without the ego demanding a "Production Report." If you cannot sit still, you are still a prisoner of the "Social Clog."

5. THE INVISIBLE GENERAL: THE SOVEREIGN GHOST STATUS

Visibility is a target. The Sovereign is a Ghost. To achieve this, you must undergo the 48-Hour Extraction Audit. Victory is measured by the length of your silence. If you cannot exist within your own skin—with nothing but a glass of water and your own thoughts—for 48 hours, you are still renting your reality from the Clog.

THE EXTRACTION TIMELINE (THE GHOST'S BAPTISM):

0–4 HOURS: Clearing the "Grey Dust" of the Mirage. 4–12 HOURS: The "Robot" begins to panic, feeling the phantom itch for distraction. 24 HOURS: The Pleasure of NOT Eating merges with the Art of Doing Nothing. The blood thins, the mind sharpens, and the Clog begins to dissolve. 48 HOURS: Sovereign Ghost Status. You no longer communicate with the world to know you own your place in it. You are the one who built the Fortress.

6. STRUCTURAL MINIMALISM: THE 30-MINUTE UPKEEP

A P.I.G. (Passive Income Generator) that requires 40 hours a week is not an asset—it is a Job in Disguise. In the Zenith, the upkeep of your fortress is limited to 30 minutes a week. The machine is built to be self-regulating. You monitor the "Milk", check the pressure in the "Artery", and then you close the ledger. Anything more is a Mechanical Failure of your design.

7. THE YIELD OF THE RIND: THE CHAOURCE PROTOCOL

The Zenith is not about asceticism; it is about Pristine Quality of Sustenance. You use the "Milk" (the profit) to buy the Chaource. You don't buy the "Mirage" of the $8 Latte; you buy the pure, organic excellence of the earth. You consume only that which resonates with your Porcelain DNA. You reward the Architect with the best, because the Architect has secured the Margin.

8. GEOGRAPHIC SOVEREIGNTY:
THE SANARY STATION

The Zenith requires an environment that matches your internal frequency. For the General, it is Sanary-sur-Mer. The blue of the water, the rhythm of the port, and the absence of the "Parisian Fog". You choose the coordinates where the "Social Clog" is thinnest and the "Organic Truth" is loudest.

9. THE LIQUIDATION OF APOLOGY:
THE SOVEREIGN "NO"

The Zenith is sustained by the word "No." You owe no explanations to the "Robots," no apologies to the "Vultures," and no "Our Fathers" to the "Mother Goose." You are the Final Authority of your own life. Your silence is your shield, and your "No" is your sword.

10. THE SUPREMACY OF THE SMALL NUMBERS: MATH AS THE ONLY MESSIAH

"Thou shalt not" is the language of the Slave. "The Math is" is the language of the Sovereign. In the Zenith, Hope is Dead, replaced by the Calculated Result. The Mythical Law: "Thou shalt not covet." (A command to ignore biology). The Sovereign Law: "The Math is $1.00 → $2.50" (A command to own the Artery so coveting becomes irrelevant). If your ledger is balanced and your 3 P.I.G.s are fed, your conscience is naturally Hygienic. The Math doesn't require "Faith"; it only requires Execution.

The Artery is not about brilliance; it is about Hygiene. Most 'Titans' fall because they allow the 'Social Clog' to re-infect them with greed or vanity.

My promise to you is simple:

Don't do anything stupid and you will be rich forever.

What is 'Stupid'?

The Assessment Error: Thinking you can 'afford' the $8 Latte because you have $20 in your pocket. In reality, you cannot afford it until your P.I.G.s are paying for it. Until then, you are eating your own 'Future Metal'.

The 'Affordability Mirage': Buying a $6 coffee because you only see the 'Small Number.' The Robot assesses the price; the Sovereign assesses the Opportunity Cost. That $6 is a soldier that should be guarding your 1st P.I.G. . Every 'Small Number' wasted is a brick removed from your own wall.

The Equity Cannibal: Taking a loan against the equity of your home or asset to fund a vacation. You are literally 'Cannibalizing the Fortress'—bleeding the walls of your sanctuary to buy a temporary Mirage. You are trading a permanent Artery for a week of 'Social Dust'.

The Unrealized Mirage: Changing your spending habits because your stocks or assets went up in value on a screen. You are spending 'Paper Heat' that hasn't been extracted into the ledger. You are counting soldiers before the battle is won, forgetting that the market can suffer a 'Mechanical Failure' before you even wake up the next morning.

Trusting the 'Ink' of a Vulture: Signing any contract that siphons your time or your metal to a 'Clerk.' The

Timeshare Trap is the perfect example—you are signing a lifelong commitment to pay for a 'Shiny Object' you don't own and don’t need... and it’s not even shiny.

The Credit Card Noose: Using 'Plastic Air' to fund a lifestyle of status symbols you haven't earned. You end up dying in debt to a card to maintain a cage you can never leave.

Buying 'The Shiny Trap' (the Gilded Cage): “Investing” in the appearance of wealth before the 3 P.IG. s are birthed. Master the 3 P.I.G.s, maintain your Sovereign Ghost status, and never let the 'Mirage' tell you that you need more than the Sanary Zenith.

I am not just shouting at you; I am providing the new operating system for your mind. Defining concepts like the "Unrealized Mirage" provides you with a razor-sharp radar for identifying hidden financial traps. Naming a parasitic behavior is always the first strike toward destroying it; once a trap is clearly dragged into the light, it becomes a visible target on your screen rather than an unconscious habit. Hunting down recurring daily leaks—like that unconscious $8 purchase—is how you master the absolute law of opportunity cost. When the cumulative power of those tiny, stolen small numbers is projected over the long term, the raw potential for growth is staggering. Do not stop at daily habits. Identify and ruthlessly execute every other financial leak in your perimeter—whether it is unused subscriptions or high-interest plastic air. Plug the holes in the wall. Deploying these strategic blueprints forces you to stop reacting blindly and start manipulating your resources with absolute intent. Clear, actionable definitions serve as an unshakeable foundation for anyone determined to master their financial hygiene and lock down long-term stability.

XI. THE GRATITUDE ARTERY: THE YIELD OF THE ANCESTRAL FORGE

I am profoundly grateful for the 1915 Logic, the ancient, unshakeable code of my grandfather, Levon. I thank him for showing me through my Father Berj that a Merchant is not defined by his office, but by his Margin. He gave me the eyes to see the 'Small Numbers' in a world obsessed with 'Big Mirages.' Without his silent guidance, I might have become just another 'Academic Robot' lost in the gears. I am grateful for the First Departure, the moment I stepped away from the 'Safe Path' and into the unknown. I thank the fear I felt then, for it was the first sign that my Biological Alarm was working. It taught me that the only true safety is found in the Artery, not in the 'Permission Slip' of an institution. I am grateful for the Social Fog of my early years. I thank the 'Clerks' and the 'Printers of the Lie' who tried to convince me that my worth was tied to a title. Their density made my exit necessary; their

'Grey Dust' made the 'Clean Gold' of sovereignty look like the only sun worth following. I am grateful for the Hard Way, the initial struggle that demanded I trade my sweat for my freedom. I thank the 'Red Dot' that was already forming in my mind—the realization that if I didn't own the pot of paint, I would be the brush forever. Finally, I am grateful for the Porcelain DNA, the resilient core that refused to break when the world tried to bend me. I am grateful to have found the path to the Sanary Zenith by honoring the simple, brutal truths of the past.

The Artery is open. The legacy is anchored. BLISS.

CHAPTER 2: THE ANCESTRAL LEDGER

2.1 THE FURNACE AND THE FORGE (THE FIRST LAW)

The First Law of the Sovereign: Wealth is not what you show; it is the hidden density that allows you to move when the world is on fire.

In 1915, the "Social Clog" didn't just fail; it turned into a furnace. One and a half million Armenian souls were slaughtered; their lands seized, their titles erased, and their "Printed Lies" incinerated by the winds of genocide. This was the ultimate Merciless Fire —the moment the world realized that paper wealth is a Mirage. While others clung to their heavy furniture and stone houses— becoming anchors for their own destruction—my grandfather, Levon Der Boghossian, prepared for the Sovereign Glitch. He understood that a Sovereign carries his vault within his stride. He realized that the only way to survive the "Printers of Death" was to become invisible to their sensors while remaining anchored in Hidden Density.

2.2 THE HERBOLOGIST'S RATIO (THE MOVING TREASURY)

Levon was a landowner and a herbologist. He understood the "Small Numbers" of the earth—the exact chemical ratio required for a plant to thrive and the exact financial ratio required for a man to survive. He knew that a seed, if dense enough, can survive a drought that kills a forest. He performed a masterclass in Financial Autophagy. Long before the "Robots" of Wall Street invented their jargon, Levon stripped away the "Fat" of his life until only the "Bone" remained. He hollowed out his weathered wooden walking cane with the precision of a surgeon. Inside that wood, he cached a supply of Gold Coins. The Rhythmic Audit: When the soldiers came, they saw a broken refugee—a man stripped of his "Clog." They let him pass because they were looking for wealth in the obvious places. They didn't understand the Algorithm of the Hidden. Levon wasn't just walking; he was a Sovereign Merchant in transit. With every rhythmic thud... thud... thud... of that cane on the dry earth, he was calculating the interest on his future freedom. He carried his bank in his hand. The cane was the first P.I.G. of our line. It didn't produce rent; it produced Survival Equity.

2.3 THE FORTRESS OF BOURJ HAMMOUD (THE 1957 BIRTH)

By the time the survivors reached the Armenian enclave of Bourj Hammoud in Beirut, the "Cane Gold" was ready to be deployed. Levon did not spend his liquid density on "Status." He bought the only thing a Sovereign respects: The Ground. He built a three story fortress of stone and brick—the Der Boghossian Building. It was a physical statement: You can seize the map, but you cannot seize the

Architect. I was not born in a hospital; in 1957 Lebanon, hospitals were for "Robots" who needed institutional validation. I was born at home, within those thick stone walls. My very entrance into the world was decoupled from the institutional "Clog". I was born a General of the Small Numbers.

2.4 ECONOMIC HYGIENE: THE FATHER'S SACRIFICE

(Dismantling the Scarcity Myth)

I was raised by my parents, Alice and Berj, first-generation survivors. My father understood Economic Hygiene with surgical clarity. He was a man of Zero Waste. He sacrificed every "Ego-Spike"—every unnecessary café coffee, every vanity vacation, every hollow designer suit meant to impress a neighbor who didn't care. He lived the absolute Protocol: Starve the Ego to Feed the

Empire. While other fathers were chasing FOMO to impress the local Vultures, mine was building the lung capacity of a dynasty. He taught me that a Merchant's pride is never measured by the size of his car, but by the unbreakable, unyielding nature of his Word. But do not let your programming mistake his Economic Hygiene for the pathetic, fearful stinginess of a clerk. The Young Vasken must understand that pinching pennies out of fear is a software glitch of the Clog; my father starved his vanity precisely so that true abundance could flow completely unrestricted to his family and his people. He was a man of immense, ferocious generosity. He protected and helped the poor no matter how much deep-sea market pressure or financial stress he was operating under. In good days and in brutal days, he gave. He was simply repeating the frequency of his own father, Levon. When Levon successfully fled a merciless genocide and arrived as a refugee in Lebanon, the very first directive he executed after raising the stone walls of the Der Boghossian

Building was to heal the needy. He deployed his ancient curing skills—an ancestral biochemical knowledge that had no official name then, but what the corporate academy today labels "homeopathy"—to cure and restore the vulnerable completely for free. Inside our fortress, my father insisted there was no limit to what we could consume. The fridge and the pantry were a sovereign territory of endless nourishment; the concept of food scarcity did not exist. He would routinely stop the car on the side of the road and buy fresh produce not by the handful, but by the heavy, raw case; mandarines, mulberries, apples, apricots, peaches, and grapes. It was an ordinary standard in our home to have five to ten varieties of seasonal fruit in massive, rolling abundance at all times. He gave fiercely to the world, often giving even when his own ledger lacked the immediate means to do so. Because of this unyielding blueprint, my two siblings and I grew up to be intentionally and profoundly generous. We help anyone we can, within our capacity, under any and all circumstances, because we carry the exact same Porcelain DNA. I do not worship material possessions like my rich friends do. I watch those heirs; unstable robots who inherited a shitload of money from their parents, yet count pennies in the dark, paralyzed by the fear of loss. They are rich on paper but utterly bankrupt in spirit. Life has taught me to unlearn their printed lies and trust the mathematical inevitability of the Universal Ledger. When you operate from the true Donor Side with an open hand, the Karma balances itself with absolute precision. Life is good

2.5 THE QUENCHING OF THE GHOST (THE SOVEREIGN EDGE)

To the "Social Clog," a glowing, visible piece of metal is a target for the hammer. Your Invisibility is the Quenching Process. By withdrawing into the Stealth

Presence of the Sanary Zenith, you are plunging your spirit into the cold water of Autonomy. The result? The metal hardens. The Slag—the Ancestral Trap and the Gilded Clog—falls away. You become a Sovereign Ghost— sharp, cold, and invisible to the Vultures. You no longer glow for their cameras or soften for their sermons. You are the Architect of the Edge, and your silence is the proof that the Forge is finally yours.

CHAPTER 3: THE LEYSIN ARBITRAGE (THE $64,000 HACK)

3.1 THE FORGED BRIDGE: FROM THE FLOOR TO THE PEAK

The student from the Citroën factory had become the Master of the Mountain, but the ascent was not a gift from the heavens; it was an Irrevocable Transformation of the Soul.

Those 2,000 Francs I had extracted from the Citroën factory floor—earned one Red Dot at a time—were the literal Sacrificial Fuel that bought my ticket to the mountain. This is a critical distinction for any "Robot" seeking the exit: You do not wait for a "Permission Slip" to climb. You forge your own key with the metal you've saved from the grind.

While the "Rich Kids" arrived in Leysin with soft hands and academic maps provided by their fathers, I arrived with the metallic taste of Paris still on my tongue. I carried the smell of the Citroën oil in my pores to the thin, elite air of the Alps. It was a biological reminder of where I had been and why I could never go back. To my classmates, the mountain was a "View"—a backdrop for their social dramas. To me, the mountain was the Artery. They were there to spend their inheritance; I was there to perform a long-range Sovereign Extraction of my own future.

3.2 THE GATEKEEPER OF LES FRÊNES

At the American College of Switzerland (ACS), I didn't just inhabit the space; I monitored the flow. I was the "Gatekeeper of Les Frênes," sitting at the reception desk where the heavy grey plastic of the switchboard phone became an electronic extension of my arm.

I remember the calls from Miami. Mme De Gonzi. Her voice was the sound of impatient wealth—a woman who expected the world to bend to her dial.

'Find my daughter', she would insist. I would let the phone ring on the third floor, the sound echoing through the sterile hallways of the dorm. I knew Martina wasn't there. In a move of 'Strict Catholic Defiance', she had secretly moved in with me, keeping her room as a "Formal Ghost" to satisfy the school's records.

As I told Mme. De Gonzi, "No one is answering, Madame", I felt the weight of the secret. I loved Martina, but I saw the "Worlds Apart" between us. My mother was a woman of the factory—soft-hearted but steel-boned. Martina was a woman of "Brand Names". I was a "Maker" in love with a "Consumer". I was paying my tuition while her peers were trying to figure out if they could buy their degrees to avoid the "humiliation" of a three-hour exam. I was learning the first hard lesson of the mountain: Love is a Bridge, but Logic is the Foundation.

3.3 THE SARDINE ARTERY:
THE METABOLIC MARGIN

My dorm room at L'Esplanade was not a place of leisure; it was a Forward Operating Base. While the sons of diplomats decorated their walls with posters of Ferraris, my room was stripped to the essentials. The most important feature was the Window Sill. In the winter, the outside air was a permanent deep freeze—my natural refrigerator. On that sill, I stacked my rations: Tins of wild caught Portuguese Sardines in extra virgin olive oil, pure Omega 3.

The Economics of the Key was my first lesson in raw efficiency. Every evening, while the "Rich Kids" headed to the local Café de Leysin to spend 25 Francs on a heavy fondue that could only be eaten by consuming mountains of heavy bread, I performed the Ritual of the Key. I would roll back the lid—click, click, click—and eat the pure, zero-carb protein.
I wasn't just eating; I was Recapitalizing.

The Rich Kid's Meal: 25 Francs. Heavy, slow, and expensive. A massive influx of high-carb lethargy that grounded their brains in the social fog. They were eating their fathers' time.

The Merchant's Meal: 1 Franc. Fast, concentrated, and independent. Pure, zero-carb fuel that kept the mind razor-sharp and ready for the glitch hunt.
The 24-Franc Margin:

Every can of sardines was a 24-Franc victory. While my peers were building a "Social Clog" of cheese, carbs, and lethargy, I was becoming leaner and more predatory. My daily margin was exactly 24 Francs—a seemingly insignificant "Small Number" that, when multiplied by 30 days, compounded into 720 Francs a month for my War Chest.

I realized then that Wealth is the distance between what you earn and what you need to survive. By keeping my survival cost at 1 franc, I was technically richer than the heirs who needed 50 francs just to feel "normal".

3.4 THE LIBRARY LABYRINTH: DR. PECK'S TEMPLE

When I wasn't at the desk or on the mat, I was in the library; the "Sacred Temple for Intellect-Hungry Geeks." The air was thick with the smell of old paper and "Clan" pipe tobacco.

Dr. Dwight Peck, the "Hippy Librarian", was a man of quiet addictions. His fingers were stained with tobacco; his teeth dark with the price of his habit.

I watched him through the dust motes dancing in the Swiss sunlight and realized that Addiction is the Enemy of Sovereignty. Whether it was Peck's pipe or my friends' reliance on their fathers' money, they were all "Chained." I mastered the Index Cards. My handwriting, once unruly, became monastic. I learned the Rhythm of the Alphabet. I was "Learning and Earning," while the sons of politicians and oil tycoons sat in the back. They didn't understand that in the Library, as in the Market, The Order is the Law.

3.5 THE $64,000 HACK: THE LAWSON DEAL

To the "Academic", a college degree is a credential. To the Sovereign Merchant, college is the first marketplace. Tuition was a wall I couldn't climb with sardines alone. I walked into the office of Richard Lawson, the Registrar. I didn't go as an applicant; I went as a Broker.

I performed a Forensic Audit of the school's empty seats. I told Lawson: "I can fill your seats. I have the contacts in the Armenian and Lebanese communities. But I want my tuition erased". We shook hands on a "Merchant's Deal". We had Dr Horn's blessing, he was the college president. I negotiated a one-time commission of 8,000 CHF for every new student I recruited—a credit applied directly to the bloodline of my education, the tuition.

I recruited eight students—Tam, Omar, Sam, Ara, and four others the next year. Every enrollment was a bayonet charge against my debt. By the time I graduated, the $64,000 wall had been dismantled. I didn't just attend the school; I Liquidated it. I didn't need a wire transfer from a father; I had a Commission Engine that I had built.

3.6 THE HUSTLER'S ECHO: STALLONE & THE MAGIC MOUNTAIN

The mountain rewarded those who looked for the Artery. I never met Sylvester Stallone, but his ghost hung over the dorms at L'Esplanade like lingering smoke. He was the original "Hard Way" archetype. The guys told me how they used to bribe him with 5 CHF when he worked the night door. Sly wasn't a "Star" then; he was a Merchant of Opportunity. He understood that a "Rule" was just a barrier with a market rate. He taught me that Rules are for those who don’t know how to negotiate.

When Hollywood arrived to film 'The Magic Mountain' of Thomas Mann, I saw another extraction point. The director needed someone to ride a vintage World War I military bicycle—a beast of heavy steel and rod brakes , that only moves forward. The "Pretty Boys" of ACS wobbled and failed. I stepped up. I had the Hands of the Citroën Factory. I didn't ask the bike for permission; I commanded it. For 100 CHF a day, I played a soldier from the past to fund my future. I proved that the "Hard Way" always wins when the terrain gets heavy.

3.7 THE DOJO ANNEXATION:

THE OLYMPIC SIGNAL

Sovereignty is about Momentum. When our South African Tae Kwon Do instructor, Erin, left for a long trip to his home in Johannesburg , he handed me the keys to the class. He thought he was leaving a 'substitute'. He was actually handing his territory to a General.

I pushed the students through 45-minute 'Monolithic Grinds'—warm-ups designed to burn the 'Academic Filth' out of their systems. The class didn't just grow; it Exploded. We moved the operation to the Leysin Sports Center, a municipal landmark overlooking a village of 3,000 humans and 10,000 cows. Among those sweat-soaked on the mats beside me, pushing through the intensity, was Silvio Giobellina.

Silvio wasn't a spectator; he was a participant who inhabited the grind. He was the future Olympic Gold Medalist, the Captain of the Swiss 4-Men bobsled team. He came from a lineage of 'Makers', In their barn at the family chalet in Leysin, they kept the sleds—the heavy, cold machinery of speed. His father was the silent engine behind the Champion, the man whose hands mastered the Aerodynamics and forged the sharp, long, shiny blades that would eventually bring the Gold home.

Silvio recognized the 'Pure Signal' of our training—a frequency of discipline that only a man destined for the podium could truly crave. He didn't just 'attend' my sessions; he respected the Sovereign Authority of the protocol. It was a defining moment. Having a future Olympic champion validate the value of my 'Hard Way' was the proof that the Citroën Floor had given me a weapon that worked at the highest levels of human performance.

I wasn't just teaching a class; I was refining the elite.

CHAPTER 4:

THE RIYADH PRESSURE COOKER

THE THERMAL ASSAULT

The transition from the "Swiss Mirage" to the Desert Forge was not a move; it was a physical assault. One moment I was in the crisp, antiseptic air of Leysin; the next, I stepped off the plane in Riyadh and the heat hit me like a blow to the chest. My sunglasses immediately blurred—the condensation of two worlds colliding. I was 24 years old. I had the Porcelain DNA of my grandfather and the 1-Franc Discipline of the Alps, but I was standing on a floor made of burning sand. This was the Riyadh Pressure Cooker—1,600 days of absolute compression designed to turn the "Carbon" of a student into the Diamond of a Maker.

THE REAR-SEAT REVELATION

A driver was waiting for me—a man from New Delhi who had traded his pride for 3,000 Rials to be a king in his village but a ghost in the Kingdom. My instinct, forged in the egalitarian cafes of Geneva, was to sit in the front. But the seat was pushed forward—a silent, rigid reminder of the hierarchy. The "Director" of the Kingdom had already set the stage. I sat in the back. I realized that to own the system, you must first understand its Mechanical Boundaries. I was a passenger in a machine I didn't yet own, but I was already performing a Incisive Audit of the power dynamics.

THE OCTAGON & THE TELEX STRIKE

PART 1 : THE DUMEZ INTERVIEW

The heart of the project was the Octagon—a massive architectural temple of efficiency where architecture, engineering, HVAC, and procurement were the spokes of the wheel. I sat across from *Jean Claude Barreau*, a "Robot of the Clog" who valued titles and procedures. I sat there as a man who spoke and wrote five languages. In the middle of our talk, M. Christian Hardoin walked in with a yellow telex—the mechanical heartbeat of 1982 business. They had a "Glitch": their translator was missing, and Mr John Anderson, an English engineer, was demanding a ten-day delay.

PART 2 :

THE TELEX STRIKE & PASSPORT CAPTURE

Barreau thrust the paper at me. I didn't hesitate. I read the English and, with the precision of an Intellectual Poet, translated it into fluent, elegant French. In ten seconds, I filled the void. I was no longer a "candidate"; I was a Tool they couldn't afford to lose. I leaned in: *"I accept your 10,000 Rials, but I want four return tickets per year to Switzerland, paid by Dumez."* Barreau stormed into the adjacent office of Paul Sonzini, the Project Manager. Through the thin walls of the Dumez headquarters, I could hear the muffled vibration of two "Printers" negotiating the terms of a new reality.

When Barreau returned, his face was a study in Sovereign Arbitrage. He wore the mask of a defeated man—the slumped shoulders of a manager who had just caved to my "Geneva Condition" of four return tickets per year— one every 10 weeks —but deep in his eyes was the glimmer of a winner. He had surrendered the "Small Numbers" of the travel budget because he realized that without my Porcelain DNA on the ground, his project was a sinking ship. He saw the tool he desperately needed, and he was willing to pay the "Tax" to secure it.

"Give me your passport," Barreau snapped. "HR will prepare the documents."

In that ten-second "Glitch", I had anchored my life to a 4.5-year Artery. The deal was sealed: four return tickets to Geneva per year, allowing me to breathe the Swiss air while the Saudi heat funded my future. But the extraction went deeper than travel.

I was moved into a state of Absolute Zero Friction. I was *nourri, logé, blanchi*—fed, housed, and my laundry handled by the Corporate Machine. Dumez provided me with a private villa, a sanctuary of stone and silence in the desert, all to myself, located in the upscale Dumez PBNG compound.

To the "Academic Robot," this looked like a luxury perk or a high-status reward. To the Merchant-General, it was the total excision of the Social Clog of daily existence. When you no longer have to hunt for food, manage a household, or navigate the mundane friction of survival, your mind becomes a razor-sharp laser focused exclusively on the Stone. My villa was not a home; it was a Forward Operating Base where I calculated my markups and monitored the pulse of my growing fortress. I was a Sovereign

Ghost in a gilded desert, and the Octagon was paying for the sanctuary that would eventually ensure my escape.

PART 3 : THE BRIDGE & THE $8,000,000 SALAD

THE INVISIBLE BRIDGE

At 24, I was the Procurement Manager for DUMEZ, overseeing a 360-building empire. My door became the "Confessional of the Clog". Senior French managers would knock in secret, terrified of the "Printer's Shame"—they couldn't write a telex in English or even master their own French properly. I corrected their words, their contracts, and their logic. I was the Linguistic Artery. I realized then that Communication is the ultimate Leverage. While they hid their ignorance, I was building a "Poker Face" of sovereignty.

THE $8,000,000 MISCALCULATION

The desert demanded a "Mirage" to keep the Robots sane. We were fed foie gras by Alsatian chefs while the sand stretched to infinity. Then came the Landscaping Audit. Following the term of out contract with the Saudi National Guard , we spent $8,000,000 on baby palms from Morocco and rare cacti from Mexico. It was a botanical miracle—an $8 million salad tossed in the middle of a wasteland.

The day of delivery arrived. The ribbon was cut. Then the Bedouin National Guard moved in with their camels, goats, and sheep. Within 24 hours, the $8,000,000 miracle was gone.

Ironclad Lesson : If you don't understand the "Small Numbers" of the environment, your "Big Numbers" will be eaten by the goats.

PART 4 : THE 1,600-DAY FAST & GRATITUDE

THE 1,600-DAY FAST

I watched the $8 million evaporate and didn't flinch. My "Clean Gold" was in my Artery. Earning 10,000 Rials with zero expenses meant 95% of my income was Liquid Dry Powder. I was conducting a 1,600-Day Fast.

I wasn't there to "live", I was there to Extract. I watched the other Frenchmen waste their Rials on status and imported distractions. I kept my eyes on the telex. Every "Click-Click-Click" of the machine was the sound of my future sovereignty.

TACTICAL CHART: THE 1,600-DAY EXTRACTION THE VELOCITY AUDIT

MONTHLY INCOME: 10,000 Rials

The Detail: Includes Flight Tickets.

The Status: Maximum Inflow.

LIVING EXPENSES: 0 Rials

The Detail: Dumez Paid (Foie Gras & Housing Inc.).

The Status: Zero Leakage.

LIQUIDITY VELOCITY: 100% Extraction

The Detail: Zero Leakage.

The Status: Absolute Sovereignty.

THE YIELD OF THANKS

I am profoundly grateful for the Riyadh Heat, for it taught me the value of the Artery. I am grateful for Paul Sonzini, who saw the General behind the translator. I am grateful for the Goats, for they showed me the futility of "Big Number" mirages. I am grateful for the 1,600-Day Fast that built the foundation of my future fortress.

CHAPTER 5

THE EXIT FROM THE OCTAGON

I walked out of the Riyadh Octagon for the last time with the Passport of a Free Man and a bank account heavy with "Clean Gold." I was 28 years old, and I had more liquid capital than 99% of the "Academic Robots" in Europe.

But I had a "Glitch" in my software. I thought the Artery would flow forever because I was "Vasken the Manager". I didn't realize that without a P.I.G., I was just a man with a finite pile of sand. I flew to London, not as a Merchant looking for a floor, but as a "Grand Seigneur" looking for a stage. This was the beginning of the great Liquidation Mirage.

THE BURGUNDY MISHAP & NEGATIVE AUTOPHAGY

London was my High-Altitude Mirage. I lived in South Kensington, surrounded by the "Social Fog" of old money. I was burning through my Saudi capital at a terrifying velocity, trading my Life Force for an "Image."

The Anesthetized Robot: One morning, I woke up and found a receipt from the H.R. Owen Range Rover Dealership. I had no memory of the transaction. The day before, I had been under the heavy I.V. anesthesia of my dentist, Dr. Wilkinson, on 10 Thurloe Street. While in a chemical haze, my Status Ego had taken the wheel. I had walked into the dealership and bought a top-of-the-line Range Rover—Burgundy exterior, tan leather, and a massive sunroof, all in Swiss Specifications. I was an idiot, purchasing a moving liability while I couldn't even remember my own name.

The Deep-Sea Pressure: By month 12, the "Clean Gold" was thin. I was experiencing Negative Financial Autophagy—my lifestyle was eating my foundation. In the true Orazon Protocol, Autophagy is the body consuming its waste to become stronger; here, it was the "Waste" (the lifestyle) consuming the "Strength" (the capital). I owned a Burgundy Range Rover and a Swiss Penthouse, but I was spiritually and financially suffocating.

THE MONTREAL BAPTISM / THE RETAIL TRAP

In 1987, I landed in Montreal with the Last Breath of my financial life. The "Swiss Mirage" evaporated the moment I felt the grey, dirty slush of a Quebec winter under my shoes.

The Merchant's Illusion: I arrived with a desperate plan. I thought I could "Trade" my way back to the top. I secured a space in Les Terrasses, the high-traffic mall of downtown Montreal. I opened three retail extraction points:

L'Orientaliste: A gallery of artcraft and collectibles from the "Far Places".

Coupe De Ville (Boutique 1 & 2): Two high-end boutiques selling European Haute Couture.

I thought I was being a Merchant. I was wrong. I was still a Robot in a Designer Suit.

I knew how to "Manage" a store, but I didn't know how to Make Money. I had the inventory, the location, and the "Image", but I lacked the Sardine Logic. I was paying high rent to a "Clerk" landlord and salaries to "Robots", all while my own capital was bleeding out into the Montreal slush.

The transition from a "High-Earning Slave" to a "Sovereign Merchant" was not the easy pivot I had imagined. I noticed too late that I was still painting "Red Dots"—only now, the dots were the price tags on clothes I couldn't afford to keep.

The Absolute Zero: That was the end of the spending streak. The bank seized the Leysin penthouse; they didn't care about the Gilles Eden design, the monumental H-shaped fireplace crafted from imported Italian Carrara Paonazzo marble, the Delepine gold-plated bathroom fixtures, or the custom turbo pump that brought hot water to the shower nozzle in under three seconds. I lost the stage, the "Face", and the gold. I was Dead Broke. I was a "Senior Manager" who couldn't pay his rent.

THE PERSIAN GLITCH: THE $10,000 CASH STRIKE

Standing in the grey, freezing slush of downtown Montreal, L'Orientaliste was bleeding capital. I was technically dead broke on paper, unable to meet the retail rent, but a Merchant-General always keeps a hidden reservoir of survival fuel. I had the prime coordinates in Les Terrasses, but I was still thinking like a high-status clerk, trying to sell luxury to a market locked in deep-sea economic pressure. I needed an immediate cash-flow volcano. I needed an asset with infinite velocity that could breathe life into the store's lungs. Then, I spotted the Glitch Floor.

A supplier was sitting on a mountain of handmade silk Persian rugs. These were truly gorgeous, high-finesse pieces of art that carried a full retail price of $500 and up on the open market. But the supplier had a logistical nightmare: the lot had slight, microscopic defects, and he was choked by the inventory volume. He didn't need "audits" or "credit lines"—he needed immediate liquidity. I applied the primary law of forensic acquisition: Buy lower than low.

I negotiated his panic down to $10 a rug. But there were two catches that would have paralyzed an academic mind: the slight imperfections, and a rigid minimum order quantity of 1,000 pieces. To execute the strike, I needed $10,000 in cold, hard cash right on the table. No notaries, no delays.

That was the wall. Cash is the ultimate King when the terrain gets heavy. I scraped the absolute bottom of the barrel—liquidating my last personal assets, emptying the dying cash drawers of the Coupe De Ville boutiques, and clawing together every loose dollar left in my perimeter to assemble that desperate, final $10,000 war chest.

I dropped the capital, loaded the inventory, and set the trap.

I didn't mark them down to a standard wholesale rate. I displayed them proudly at $200 each—a colossal 80% discount off full retail for my clients, yet a staggeringly healthy markup for my ledger. When the clients walked into L'Orientaliste, looking closely at the exquisite weave, they would inevitably spot the slight variations. That is when I deployed the linguistic shield. I looked them in the eye and delivered the frame:

"The master artist who wove this rug by hand is a true believer. Because of his deep humility, he chose to leave a deliberate imperfection in the silk. He did this out of profound respect, refusing to challenge the absolute perfection of the Almighty with a flawless human creation."

The frame was unyielding. The imperfection wasn't a defect anymore; it was the sacred stamp of authenticity, elite craftsmanship, and made each rug "unique" in the true sense.

The clients didn't just buy the rugs—they bought two or four at a time, completely euphoric to possess a holy piece of history at a fraction of the regular retail price. A truly amazing value for money.

This was the architecture of the Triple-Win Artery in

its purest form. The supplier got his clean extraction, the client got a magnificent handmade silk treasure for 80% off, and the Merchant extracted a massive yield to reinforce the fortress.

Opportunities like this do not come often, but when the glitch appears, only the General with immediate dry powder has the speed to annex the terrain.

THE DEATH OF LES TERRASSES , THE MONTREAL DOWNTOWN MALL

THE UNINTENTIONAL LAUNCHPAD

The Persian rug strike was the literal oxygen for *L'Orientaliste*. By injecting that raw 2,000% narrative margin into the ledger, I was on the cusp of refining that gallery into a highly optimized, permanently profitable retail engine. I had the math, I had the cash-flow velocity, and I had the consumer frequency. But the "Social Clog" has a way of moving its heavy, bureaucratic gears behind your back.

The year was 1987. The institutional planners of Montreal had already signed the execution orders for the physical terrain under my feet. Les Terrasses—the very artery where my shop breathed—was targeted for a planned, systematic demolition to be replaced by what is now the corporate monolith of The Eaton Center. To a linear consumer mind, having your retail location flattened by a wrecking ball looks like an absolute tragedy. They see a closed door; they see the end of a track. But the Sovereign General knows that when the system forces a liquidation, it is merely clearing your schedule for a massive tactical upgrade. Had Les Terrasses been spared, I might have spent a decade as a high-performing retail prisoner, managing a successful storefront inside a corporate matrix. Instead, the universe used their wrecking balls to perform a Brutal Eviction on my lifestyle.

The closure of *L'Orientaliste* stripped me down to absolute zero baseline. It pushed me out of the shiny commercial complexes and forced my feet onto the freezing, historic cobblestones of the Old Port of Montreal. If the city hadn't torn down that building, I would have stayed comfortable.

I would have remained blind to the parallel frequency. And most importantly, I would never have walked into the office of Mme Lise Kelly at Le Marché aux Puces du Vieux Port, the exact coordinate where my permanent renaissance was initiated. The corporate architects built their Eaton Center to harvest the wallets of the masses. But in doing so, they cast out the Maker who was about to conquer the hosiery artery of 555 Chabanel West. The ledger was clearing. The stage was being dismantled. The General was being driven under white-hot pressure straight toward his true destination.

THE GRATITUDE ARTERY

THE YIELD OF THANKS

I am profoundly grateful for the Montreal Slush, the cold reality that killed my Ego and allowed me to finally become a Maker. I am grateful to be Clean, back at zero, ready to turn $1.00 into $2.50. I am grateful for the "Grey Winter", for it taught me that the only true "Sun" is the one you print for yourself in your own Ledger.

VOLUME II: THE FORGE

CHAPTER 6

THE SILK MULTIPLIER (THE BREACH)THE BIRTH OF THE GLITCH HUNTER

Standing at zero in Montreal was the most Hygienic moment of my life. The "Filth" of my London arrogance had been burned away by the poverty.

I was no longer a "Grand Seigneur"; I was a Merchant with nothing to lose and a newly calibrated set of eyes.

The Software Update: The London Burn was a Negative Glitch—a total system failure caused by my Status Ego. But as

I stood in the Montreal slush, my software underwent a radical update. I stopped being a victim of the "Printers' Glitches" and became a Hunter of Glitches.

I realized that every "Clog," every "Waiting List," and every "Rigid Rule" in the world of the Robots has a crack.

A Sovereign doesn't stand in line; he looks for the Systemic Error that allows him to bypass the line entirely.

I began to look for the "Glitch" in every room I entered. I looked for the opening that others were too "obedient" to see.

I. THE MORGUE OF AMBITION: BREACHING THE QUEUE

Mme. Lise Kelly's office was the morgue of ambition.

On her desk sat the "Ledger of the Clog"—a list of 200 names representing a three-year sentence for anyone wanting to enter the Old Port Flea Market , Le Marché aux Puces du Vieux-Port de Montréal.

" Monsieur !! " she said, her voice dripping with the stagnation of the bureaucrat, "the rules are the rules. 1990 is your window. There is no exception to the rules" She smiled with the smirk of an institution that believes it owns Time.

I realized the list was just Linguistic Friction for the weak. I walked onto the floor. I wasn't going to wait three years for a "Permission Slip" to begin my life. I was going to find the crack in the wall.

II. THE IDENTIFICATION OF JIM

(THE CLOGGED PIPE)

I performed a Structural Audit of the 15,000-person social clog. Most vendors were "Waiters," praying for customers while their energy bled into the concrete.

I looked for a "Clogged Pipe" , someone with the space but no fire. I found him: Jim. He was selling generic oil paintings and had already quit in his mind. He looked stressed.

I stepped into his space: “How much for the whole thing? The space, the paintings, the right to stand here. Right now.” “Eight thousand, eight hundred dollars”, he said, cost plus 10%.

I was dead broke on institutional credit, and the Eaton Center demolition had flattened my retail storefront, but the Vultures hadn't touched my armored perimeter. I still held the hard cash residue harvested from the Persian rug volcano.

I wrote the check on the spot. I didn't want his paintings; I wanted his Coordinates.

Twenty minutes later, I returned to Mme. Kelly's office with the signed transfer. Her smirk collapsed. I had bypassed the three-year merchant waiting list wall in thirty minutes because

I stopped looking at the "Rules" and started looking at the Flow.

III. THE DEATH OF THE STATUS EGO

I realized that I didn't need a penthouse or a Coupe De Ville storefront; I needed a Margin. I needed to move from the 'Big Numbers' that had betrayed me to the Small Numbers of the Flea Market.

The 'Social Clog' had taken my gold, but it couldn't take the 1915 Logic of my grandfather.

In the same way my sister, Sylva—whom I love and admire, a master artist in Richmond Hill, Ontario—captures the density of life through the layers of oil and acrylic on her canvases, a Sovereign must learn to Layer their Assets.

You layer them so that the truth of your wealth is visible only to those who understand the craft. I was clean, I was cold, and I was ready to start the 111-Day Burn.

IV. THE ALTAR OF THE FOLDING TABLE

In 1987, the "Swiss Mirage" of my Geneva education had evaporated, leaving me standing in the grey, bone-chilling slush of a Quebec winter.

To the "Academic Robot," I was a failure—a man with a Master's Degree standing on a street corner. But the Robot sees only the surface. I possessed the Porcelain DNA of a survivor, and I knew that an empire does not begin in a glass tower. It begins on a Folding Table. I did not look for a "Job" in the corporate Octagon.

I stepped into that human laboratory to Annex territory. The 111-Day Burn was about to begin, and this time, I wasn't painting Red Dots. I was hunting them.

VOLUME II: THE FORGE

CHAPTER 7

THE MERCHANT MACHINE (THE SCALE)

I. THE ALCHEMY OF HIGH-VELOCITY LIQUIDITY

Once the Breach was complete, I needed a Cash-Flow Volcano. I didn't want a "Boutique"; I needed a product with Infinite Velocity—something every human in the 15,000-person "Social Clog" required every single day. I found the Socks.

THE DISTINCTION: SILK VS. STONE

Before you can own the Stone (The P.I.G.), you must master the Silk (The Multiplier). SILK is for speed, accumulation, and the generation of Dry Powder.

STONE is for density, preservation, and the Sanary Zenith. The General uses the Silk to spin the "Dough" that buys the Stone.

II. THE $1.00 TO $2.50 ALGORITHM (THE MULTIPLYING SEED)

The Young Vasken asks: "How can I sell for 2.5 times my cost without hitting resistance?" Before you even look at the selling price, you must master the Law of the Buy: Don't mix emotions when you buy. If the numbers don't coincide with your pricing criteria, just walk away from the deal.

If the Seed cannot yield the Milk, the asset is actually a liability in disguise. This is the primary math of the Forge. It is an immutable mathematical strike: Seed ($): $1.00 (The Investment) Multiplier: 2.5x (The Merchant Edge) Yield (Milk): $2.50 (The Sovereign Result)

III. THE SECRET SAUCE: THE DEPTH OF THE BUY

Young Vasken, listen closely: your edge is not in the "Sale"; it is in the Forensic Acquisition. You do not buy at "Wholesale". You buy low, LOWER than low.

You must become a Hunter of the Glitch Floor. You should be looking for end-of-lines and discontinued items, but brand new and clean. “Overstock” and “Surplus” items, in market jargon.

These are the items that the "Academic Robots" in department stores currently have marked at $8.00 each.

To the department store, these items are a "Logistical Nightmare"—clogging their shelves and eating their overhead.

The Sovereign Strike:

Vasken buys it at $0.50. Vasken sells it at $2.00 each (or 3 for $5.00). The Result: Your markup is higher than 250%. You are selling at 80% off retail, yet you are extracting a 250% yield on your investment. This is the Ultimate Glitch in the world of high-velocity retail.

THE COMMAND: THE ANTIDOTE TO GREED

Young Vasken, if you get greedy here, you will stumble and fall. Seeing these massive markups and the deep 80% discount, you might be tempted to say: “Well, I can sell it at 50% off retail and it will still be a great buy for the client.”

STOP RIGHT THERE. At 50% off, you might sell well enough to pay your rent and your salaries, but you will NEVER move the volumes required to build an empire.

The key strategy is Colossal Volume. Velocity is the only way to turn a "Seed" into a "Fortress" in record time.

Greed is a venom, a self-inflicted wound, and a form of potential financial suicide. Do not choke the Artery for a few extra cents today when you could be Annexing the entire territory tomorrow.

IV. THE TRIPLE-WIN ARTERY: RETAIL EUPHORIA

How is this not a Retail High Volume, High Hype Euphoria?

THE 3-WAY GLITCH VICTORY

When you operate at the Glitch Floor, you create a 3-way victory that the Octagon cannot comprehend:

WIN 1 The Supplier : They get "Sweet Milk" (Cash) for discontinued items that would otherwise be destroyed at a high cost. You solve their nightmare.

WIN 2 The Client : They walk away with a premium product at 80% off. You provide them with a miracle of value.

WIN 3 The Merchant : You extract a 250% yield on your Seed. You secure the absolute prize.

This is not "Business"—this is Sovereign Alchemy. You are turning the "Waste" of the Robots into the "Gold" of the Sovereign.

V. THE PAUL ST. JAMES PROTOCOL (THE PACKAGING GLITCH)

The “Academic Robots” at the Doris Hosiery Mills were blinded by their own spreadsheets and marketing manuals. They saw "End-of-Line" waste—stock that didn't fit the current marketing "Sleeve".

To them, if the cardboard was slightly off-color or the branding was discontinued, the entire inventory was a "Logistical Clog." Because the packaging was "wrong," they saw garbage. I didn't look at the cardboard; I looked at the Product Sovereignty.

The women of Montreal didn’t wear the cardboard; they wore the Silk. While the Robots were calculating the cost of destroying the "waste", I was calculating the Milk. By ignoring the "Garbage" of the packaging,

I secured 50% off the Gold. I drove my wagon to the mills and walked in with the White DL Envelope of Green Queens (C$20s). I didn't want a seat at their boardroom table; I wanted the floor of their warehouse.

When we loaded the pallets, the suspension on my wagon groaned—a mechanical scream of Monumental Profit. I was turning their "Nightmare" into my "Euphoria" at the speed of cash.

VI. THE HANDSHAKE COVENANT

(THE SOVEREIGN FOUNDATION)

Paul St. James was the Clean-Cut Angel who saw in me a mirror of his own nobility. I offered him the one thing more valuable than money: Silence.

I gave my word not to wholesale and not to "Leak" his inventory to competitors, protecting his brand while I extracted my margin.

The Law of the Artery:

The deal should be good for both sides. If not, then it's not a good deal.

This is the Sovereign Foundation: a result of high-level honorable handshakes that no written contract can match.

While the "Robots" hire lawyers to draft 50-page traps filled with fine print and notaries, the Merchant-General builds on his Word.

To earn the trust of my supplier AND my clients—week in week out, month in month out, rain or shine, year in year out—this is the real grounded, genuine, and organic building of a steady-growth solid empire.

For 22 years, the envelopes of green 20s arrived every Monday morning without fail. No "Fine Print", no "Notaries", no "Ego".

Leverage comes from being the Fastest Payer. By being the Cash Fountain, I created a "Supplier's Addiction". Paul didn't call the highest bidder—he called the man who made his life easy.

He knew that when Vasken shook his hand, the math was settled, the profit was certain, and the Artery was secure.

VII. THE OLD PORT EVICTION: SMELLING THE FEDERAL GLITCH

A master merchant doesn't just listen to market reports; he listens to the pavement. I talked to everyone—the neighbors on the historic streets, the storefront owners, the homeless men warming their hands near the docks.

I kept my sensors sharp. By the late 90s, the whisper on the cobblestones turned into an undeniable signal. The Canadian Federal Government was planning a massive, multi-million-dollar aesthetic overhaul of the Old Port, transforming the Maritime Waterfront into an avant-garde tourist venue.

The first IMAX theater in Montreal was slated to rise literally adjacent to our Flea Market pavilion. The local municipal authorities and provincial powers had zero say—the quay and the piers belonged directly to the Canadian Federation.

I smelled the transition cooking long before the first shovel hit the dirt. I watched Mme. Lise Kelly closely. Every time I brought up long-term planning, her eyes darted away, her speech grew tight, and her baseline anxiety spiked.

She was operating on a high-friction, seasonal framework—renewing our coordinates one 111-day stint at a time. She knew her empire was shifting under her feet, and her humongous, overblown ego was terrified of the impending collapse.

I knew the Flea Market was never my permanent home. I refused to spend my existence sweating in gritty dust and pigeon shit. It was a trampoline, a mechanical launchpad.

While I was working that folding table and multiplying my $1.00 into $2.50, I was already in deep, strategic communication with Daniel Martin at CIBC. I was never idle.

I was mapping out the birth of my permanent P.I.G.s. All I had to do was maintain extreme discipline and avoid doing anything stupid. It was time to scale.

VIII. THE CHABANEL ANNEXATION: BYPASSING THE GATEKEEPERS

The textile capital of Montreal was 555 Chabanel West—a soaring fortress of manufacturing, wholesale, and elite distribution. It was an incredibly exclusive perimeter, heavily fortified against outsiders.

I didn't send a letter or wait for an introduction. I marched straight into mission control to find Eyal Cohen, the General Manager of the entire complex.

The moment I breached the threshold, three defensive secretaries scrambled to their feet, blocking my path like human shields. "Monsieur, you cannot enter! You do not have an appointment!" they shouted.

Hearing the commotion at his gateway, Eyal stepped out of his private office. I stood my ground, balanced on my own axis. I looked him dead in the eye: "I am Vasken, the owner of Vas & Co, a rapidly expanding Montreal retail chain".

Eyal checked his watch. He was a man of appointments, but he recognized a high-density frequency when it stood on his floor. "I have a meeting right now", he said, "but if you can give me exactly one hour, I will sit with you".

IX. THE FORTRESS OF FLAVOR: CAFFÈ GENTILE

THE GENTILE MONOLITH: THE ARCHITECTURE OF AUTHENTICITY

Right across from the landmark 555 Chabanel—the towering fashion fortress of Canada—stands a monument built on pure, unyielding grit: Caffè Gentile.

This wasn't just a business; it was a sovereign outpost of the Mediterranean transplanted into the concrete of Montreal. This was a second-generation, hard-working Sicilian dynasty that refused to compromise on the ledger of quality. They didn't just serve coffee; they served an unassailable standard. They carried the fire of their homeland in their blood, proudly stamping the legendary Sicilian flag directly into the very logo of their brand.

For decades, while the corporate franchises sold diluted, industrial dishwater to the masses, the Gentile family stood as the ultimate gatekeepers of flavor, serving the undisputed BEST coffee in the entire city. They became a landmark because they understood a truth that the "Academic Robots" will never grasp: true wealth isn't just about paper money; it is about an uncompromised legacy of excellence filled with passion and love of their roots that commands respect from the entire street.

I walked across those lanes to wait out my sixty minutes in this temple of pure passion and purpose, where coffee was treated with high-fidelity reverence. The Gentiles welcomed me not as a transient consumer, but as a brother merchant who respected the speed of their craft. To this day, they remain my close friends. Evcn now, looking back across the years from the Sanary Zenith, that bond remains completely unbroken. Literally two days ago, Paul Gentile sent a text directly to my screen: "Ciao Bello Come Stai?!" It is a brief, sharp signal, but it is the ultimate proof of human currency. When you operate with genuine passion and honor, good people remember your frequency long after you leave the territory.

Exactly one hour later, I walked back across Chabanel, bypassed the silent secretaries, and stepped into Eyal Cohen's office. We signed a fixed five-year lease for Unit R2D that very afternoon. When that lease matured, I renewed it. Then I renewed it again. My operational timeline was a masterclass in overlapping leverage.

I spent 11 consecutive years at the Old Port Flea Market, but during the final two years of that run, I ran a dual-engine operation, overlapping directly with 12 consecutive years at 555 Chabanel West. I was extracting liquidity from the pavement to permanently fund my wholesale tower.

X. THE VAS & CO OCTANE: FOUR RETAIL EXTRACTION POINTS

Unit R2D became the central beating heart, our master logistics hub and warehouse facility. From this mission control base, the silk generated from the St. James protocol was directed with absolute velocity into our expanding retail footprint.

I didn't stop at one storefront. I established a highly synchronized fleet of four corporate retail stores across the premier commercial arteries of Montreal, operating under the banner of Vas & Co. We annexed premium, high-traffic terrain inside Cours Mont Royal, established an extraction point within the elite corridors of Decarie Square Mall, and locked down two additional high-volume locations, along with a warehouse on Boulevard Henri

Bourassa.

Every single morning, the retail honey from four separate registers flowed continuously through the pipeline and directly onto my ledger.There was zero bureaucratic clog, zero corporate committee friction, and zero institutional weight. The retail chain functioned as an automated wealth generator, turning raw hosiery inventory into pure, liquid Dry Powder while I maintained absolute tactical command of the perimeter.

XI. THE RANGE ROVER GLITCH: NEVER ENVY THE CAGE

As you drive your wagon into the supplier's warehouse, do not be intimidated by the brand-new Range Rovers and BMWs in the reserved spots.

The "Academic Robot" sees success; the Sovereign sees the "Golden Handcuffs". You are liquid; they are often "Asset Rich and Cash Poor", trapped in a high-status cage.

Never trade your Porcelain DNA for their "Status Mirror". Your $20 "Green Queens" have more sovereignty than their debt-fueled fleet.

XII. THE RED MARKER LAW: LIQUIDATING FRICTION

Most vendors were trapped in the Linguistic Friction of "Tax".

I took a thick, Red Heavy Marker and wrote: “12 PAIRS FOR $10.00 – TAXES INCLUDED”.

I removed the friction of the "Cents". I didn't need a calculator; I needed a Bag. A customer hands me a $10 bill

(A Brown King). I hand them a bag. Zero Friction.

While the "Academic" vendor spent 20 minutes explaining a $50 painting, I processed 30 people for $300.

XIII. THE SUSHI STRIKE:

THE MURDER OF THE EGO

THE TATAMI AUDIT:

WHAT IS THE "SUSHI TEST"?

To understand why some of my oldest "friends" turned into robotic anchors, you must understand the Tatami Audit.

The scene was a famous, high-end Japanese restaurant in Montreal—the kind of place where the "corporate elite" gather to eat expensive sushi and perform their status dances. I was there with Tarek, Juan, Ciro, and our wives. This setting changed everything. When we were just the guys, their behavior was tolerable. But in front of their wives, the undercurrent of their insecurity turned toxic. All three of their wives openly respected me and looked up to my frequency, which drove those three husbands into a quiet, passive-aggressive madness. To make the matrix even more volatile, my then-wife was spiraling into a tailspin of bitter jealousy toward her three friends. The air in that room was thick with unspoken social friction. But Japanese tradition has a beautiful, accidental way of dismantling the Ego. We were escorted to a traditional Tatami room for dinner. In a Tatami room, the rules are absolute: you must remove your shoes before stepping onto the woven straw mats. At the threshold, the illusion shattered. Their thousand-dollar leather shoes were left on the floor, and suddenly, all eyes fell to our feet. While they wore expensive, brand-name designer socks to signal their compliance with the corporate grid, I stepped onto the mat wearing simple, unbranded, highly durable cotton socks from my own wholesale inventory. My socks were pure, functional utility, devoid of the green crocodile or the luxury logo. I watched their eyes lock onto my feet. Tarek, Juan, and Ciro sat in their corporate uniforms, staring at my basic socks as if they were a "Step Backward". They smirked. In their tiny, leased-car minds, my lack of an "Ego-Logo" on my feet meant I was failing. They desperately, pathetically needed me to be "poor" to justify the slow, agonizing drain of their own 9-to-5 incarceration. They were celebrating a "socks victory" in a luxury restaurant, completely blind to the fact that while they were servicing massive credit card debt to maintain their "image", my wholesale engines in Chabanel were dumping thousands of untaxed, clean dollars onto my ledger every single week.

For twenty-five years in Montreal, these so-called "friends" coasted on the illusion of superiority, hiding their cowardice and feeble self-confidence behind corporate titles while whispering behind my back. Their fragile egos could only exist if they believed I was struggling. They loved me as long as they thought I was down in the mud with them, but the moment the smoke cleared and my Orazon fortress appeared, their counterfeit loyalty turned to pure, green envy.

If a "friend" judges your trajectory from the passenger seat of their "Safe Ride" but lacks the spine to witness the white-hot heat of your Forge, they are not brothers, they are Robotic Anchors. They traded a quarter-century of genuine allegiance for a temporary dose of petty vanity, completely oblivious to the fact that while they were managing their cages, I was mastering the Artery. I didn't just leave the table. I cut the line forever. Let them choke on the dust of my departure.

XIV. THE 111-DAY BURN: INFINITE VELOCITY

I worked for 111 days at a time with Absolute Intensity, moving 4,400 units a week.

THE HARDWARE RESET (0-DEBT BASELINE):

Silk cannot be woven with the "Vulture's" thread. You operate with Absolute Zero Debt. If you cannot buy the inventory with your own cash, you do not move. This ensures that when the "Ass-Bite" of the market happens, you have no "Surface Area" for the banks to grab.

THE YIELD OF THANKS

(THE GRATITUDE ARTERY)

I am profoundly grateful for the Montreal Slush, the cold reality that allowed me to finally become a Maker. I am profoundly grateful for Paul St. James, the anchor of my empire. He saw the grit in the station wagon and the honor in the handshake. I am grateful for the Folding Table, the humblest altar of the Merchant. I am grateful for the 'Green Queen' ($20), the seed that I refused to eat, which eventually grew into the Orazon Fortress. I am grateful for the 'Sushi Robots'—Tarek, Juan, and Ciro. Their judgment was the high-octane fuel that drove my 111-Day Burn.

CHAPTER 8: THE AUTOPHAGY PROTOCOL
(The Mintz Liquidity & The Jamnadas Mandate)

8.1 THE RITUAL OF THE STACKS (THE MINT)

In the Orazon Protocol, money is not a digital ghost or an abstract number on a screen; it is Physical Power. To run the Forge, I became my own Mint. I realized the "Green Queen" (The Canadian $20 Bill) was the most efficient unit of commercial energy.

The Anatomy of a Brick:

- The Denomination: $20 bills.
- The Density: Exactly 50 bills per stack ($1,000).
- The Snap: Two thick rubber bands—one on each side.

The sound of that Thwack against the paper was the sound of Certainty. Ten of these bricks on a glass table represented a Financial Bypass—the ability to walk into any factory and change the priority of the loading dock. I wasn't carrying "cash"; I was carrying Oxygen for the desperate.

8.2 THE WHITE DL ENVELOPE (THE PERMISSION SLIP)

I placed five of these bricks ($5,000) into a crisp, white DL-size envelope. In the Forge, a white envelope is a Permission Slip to ignore the rules of the "Social Clog." No invoices, no "Net-30" waiting periods. I was the only man coming to the table with Immediate Liquidity. It was Liquid Powder ready to be ignited.

The Siege of Columbia Pictures (Visual Honey):

I pulled my wagon up to the empire of Neil Mintz. He sat in an office of "Steel and Glass", but he was trapped by the "Big Numbers" on his balance sheet.

He needed currency the bank didn't need to know about. I handed him the White DL Envelope; in exchange, the forklift dropped a pallet of "Visual Honey"—oil paintings and framed prints. I was buying Velocity. I was the Critical Valve that allowed his inventory to breathe while I annexed the margin.

8.3 THE FOMO GLITCH
(SOCIAL NOISE)

Before you can master the Artery, you must master the Noise. The "Social Clog" survives by injecting the FOMO Virus—the Fear Of Missing Out—into the "Receiver". It is the invisible pressure that tells you to buy the "Burgundy Mirage" or spend your Seed Capital on status symbols to impress "Robots" who are being digested by the State.

FOMO is a leak in your Porcelain DNA. It creates a state of permanent "High-Insulin Anxiety". To become a Maker, you must kill the FOMO. While the

"Robots" are afraid of missing the party, you are busy Annexing the Floor.

8.4 THE JAMNADAS MANDATE: BIOLOGICAL AUTOPHAGY

Autophagy is the biological process where a healthy body consumes its own damaged cells and waste to create new energy. In the Orazon Protocol, this is the Systemic Cleansing.

Most people are "Receivers" of glucose every four hours. Their systems are clogged with Sedative Feed leading straight into an addictive cycle (sugar and processed carbs), trapping their brains in a fog of insulin spikes. The General operates in a state of Low-Insulin Calm

8.5 THE 4 PILLARS OF THE BIOLOGICAL STRIKE

To achieve Zenith Clarity, you must cross the "Hump" and activate these four biological upgrades:

1. Autophagy (The Cellular Janitor):

After 16+ hours of fasting, your body begins a "Deep Clean." It finds old, broken proteins and "Zombie Cells" and eats them for fuel. You are recycling your own waste into high-octane energy.

2. BDNF (The Brain Fertilizer):

Fasting triggers the release of Brain-Derived Neurotrophic Factor. Think of this as "Miracle-Gro" for your neurons. It repairs old brain cells and grows new ones. This is how you achieve Mental Lasers instead of "Academic Fog".

3. HGH Surge (The Muscle Shield):

During a fast, your Human Growth Hormone can spike by up to 2,000%. This isn't just about muscle; it's about Biological Resilience. Your body is protecting its "Stone" while burning its "Fat".

4. Metabolic Flexibility (The Dual-Fuel Engine):

"Robots" can only run on Sugar (Glucose). When the sugar runs out, they crash. The OMAD Sovereign can run on Sugar or Fat (Ketones). When there is no food, your brain simply switches to your body's "On-Board Fuel Tank". You become Unstoppable.

8.6 THE BIOLOGICAL ARBITRAGE

THE POWER OF OMAD

The Great Energy Diversion:

Your body is a factory. Digestion is the most expensive department—it consumes nearly 30% of your daily energy. When you eat all day, the "Power Grid" is constantly diverted to the stomach. Your brain is running on backup generators.

By practicing OMAD (One Meal A Day), you shut down the "Digestion Department" for 22 hours. That massive surge of energy has nowhere else to go but up—into the Prefrontal Cortex. This is the "General's Room" of the brain, the place where decisions, logic, and long-term strategy are born.

8.7 MENTAL LASERS : THE PENETRATING FOCUS

Low-insulin living creates Mental Lasers. While the "Robots" are distracted by the "8-Million Dollar Salad", the Sovereign Ghost is performing a Razor-Sharp Audit of the room. This focus allowed me to spot the "Jim Glitch" in 30 minutes. You cannot have "Laser Focus" if your blood is thick with "Social Slush".

The 22-Year Hygiene:

For 22 years, I maintained the Paul St. James Protocol and the Jamnadas Mandate simultaneously. I carried the White DL Envelopes with steady hands because my nervous system wasn't vibrating on sugar and fear. I was Liquid, Light, and Lethal.

8.8 THE AUDIT: CLOGGED VS. SOVEREIGN

THE CLOGGED MIND (High Insulin)

The Driver: Driven by FOMO and Validation
The Vision: Trapped in "Academic Fog"
The Movement: Heavy, Slow, and "Digested"
The Focus: Chases the "Big Number" Mirage

THE SOVEREIGN MIND (Autophagy)

The Driver: Driven by Logic and Yield
The Vision: Operates with Mental Lasers
The Movement: Weightless, Fast, and Sovereign
The Focus: Masters the Small Numbers

8.9 THE YIELD OF THANKS

(THE GRATITUDE ARTERY)

I am profoundly grateful for the White DL Envelope, the tool that bypassed the 'Social Clog.' I am grateful for the Jamnadas Mandate, for it gave me back my eyes. I am grateful for the Fast, for it taught me that I am not a slave to my hunger or my ego.

Most of all, I am grateful for the Cleanliness—internal and external—that allows me to stand at the Zenith today. The Cash Fountain is flowing, and the Silk is turning into Stone. BLISS.

CHAPTER 9

THE COLLATERAL LOOP & THE DECARIE SIEGE

THE ACADEMIC WALL (CIBC DECARIE)

By the mid-2000s, I had been a Merchant for nearly twenty years. I had the "Cash Flow," the Rolex, and the Porcelain DNA, but to the "Academic Robots" at the bank, I was a ghost. I didn't have a T4, a corporate leash, or a predictable paystub. I walked into the CIBC on Decarie Boulevard to see the manager, Daniel Martin. My objective: To acquire two brand-new units in the Jules Poitras project. Daniel looked at my file with the eyes of a "Receiver": “Vasken, you aren’t on a payroll. Toronto will never approve this”. In the "Social Clog," this is the end. For the Sovereign Merchant, it is the invitation to find the Glitch.

THE STRATEGIC PIVOT (THE ANCHOR)

I didn’t argue with Daniel’s rules. I knew I owned 355 Berri, Apt 403, free and clear. This was the result of a 20-Year Siege.

Back in the early days, I had secured this anchor for $130,000. While the "Robots" were busy upgrading their lifestyles and chasing the "Burgundy Mirage," I was performing a Systematic and relentless Pay-down. For two decades, I stayed consistent, disciplined, and invisible. By the time I walked into CIBC, that $130,000 entry point had matured into $320,000 of Liquid Equity, right on the St Laurent river , in Historic Old Montreal .

I hadn't just saved money; I had built an Ironclad Weapon.

I had bled that mortgage down to zero until the roof over my head became the ultimate collateral.

THE COLLATERAL CONTRADICTION

(THE RENT-FIRST LAW)

I can hear the "Academic Robots" now: “Vasken, you say a primary residence is a liability, yet you used yours to build your empire. Which is it?”

My rule remains Stone: You should rent your lifestyle and buy the cow first. Use the milk of the cow to buy your shiny objects and your "Social Mirage" roof. In my case, 355 Berri #403 was a 20-year tactical evolution.

By bleeding that mortgage to zero, I didn't just "own a home"; I had decontaminated a liability. I had stopped the "Drain" and created a Dormant Cow. Most people treat their home equity like a "Social ATM" to fund vacations and Burgundy Mirages. I treated mine as a Solid Collateral.

This isn't Real Estate 101; it’s Leverage Financing. I didn't ask the bank for a mortgage to "live"; I asked them for an Extended Loan against a paid-in-full fortress to annex two more assets. I weaponized my shelter so it could finally pay for itself.

GOOD DEBT VS. BAD DEBT: THE SOVEREIGN DIVIDE

In the "Social Clog", people are taught to fear all debt. They are right to be afraid, because most of them only know Bad Debt—the kind that digests your future to pay for your present.

- Bad Debt (The Parasite):

  Borrowing to buy a status symbol, a vacation, or a "Social Mirage" that loses value while charging you interest. This is a leak in your Artery.

- Good Debt (The Fuel):

  Borrowing to acquire a self-sustaining asset. This is the "Decarie Siege" logic.

“Daniel”, I said, leaning in. “What if we don't look at my paystub ? What if we look at my Fortress ?" I wasn't looking for a loan to "spend". I was looking for Good Debt—the fuel that would allow me to annex Units #2 and #3. I was putting my $320,000 stone on the table to capture the bank’s capital.

THE ARA GLITCH
(THE COLLATERAL STACK)

Shortly after, a friend named Ara—paralyzed by "Academic Fear"—decided to back out of his commitment for [what became my] Unit #3 in the same building. He saw "Risk"; I saw a P.I.G. in Training. I didn't hesitate. I went back to the loading dock of the bank.

“Daniel, I’m taking Ara’s unit too. But this time, I’m putting two roofs on the table”. I offered the combined equity of 355 Berri and the now-free-and-clear Unit #2 as collateral for a single mortgage on Unit #3.

I had created a Collateral Loop. CIBC couldn't refuse the math. They were looking at two paid-off fortresses guaranteeing one investment. Toronto didn't just approve it; they saluted it.

THE TRIPLE-ARTERY SYSTEM

I was no longer just an owner; I was the architect of a self-sustaining machine:

- Unit 1 (355 Berri): The Original Anchor (The 20-Year Montreal Stone , and my Fortress of Discipline).
- Unit 2 (Jules Poitras): The Parental Sanctuary (Bought via the Anchor).

- Unit 3 (Jules Poitras): The Investment P.I.G. (Bought via the Double-Anchor).

Unit #3 immediately began paying for its own mortgage while harvesting equity through capital gains. I was living in

Velocity Time, using the bank's own greed to fund the extraction of my life from the Montreal slush.

But to understand why I could sit in Daniel Martin’s office with such a straight spine, you have to understand the Brutal Baptism that happened at my kitchen table years earlier. While the bank dealt in "Low-Interest Stone", my daily business was fueled by "High-Interest Fire".

THE 26% BAPTISM

VELOCITY VS. LINEAR TIME

My wife was horrified. She wasn't looking at the real estate ledgers; she was looking at the credit card statements used to finance the massive inventory strikes for the hosiery business. She saw a 26% interest rate as a financial death sentence. She was trapped in "Linear Time"—the world where you pay bills and wait for the end.

I was living in Velocity Time. I didn't argue with her emotions; I looked at the Financial Spread of the Hosiery Artery:

- The Bank's Friction: 26% Annually (roughly 2.16% per month).
- The Merchant's Strike: I was turning $1,000 into $4,000 in 30 days. That is a 400% Monthly Return.

I told her: “I am paying the bank $21.60 in interest so I can make $3,000 in profit. That is the Asymmetric Spread. I am using their 'Expensive' debt to buy my Freedom at a discount.

The standard consumer mind looks at a 26% interest rate and panics, instantly cataloging credit card leverage as 'bad debt'. They miss the weapon right in front of them. This debt is highly utile and handy, but above all, it is strictly short-term. It is a tactical bridge that ensures I never lose the opportunity to seize merchandise that is better than gold—inventory that easily multiplies a single dollar into two or more in a matter of two to three months.

This ridiculously high interest rate is completely temporary; it is taken care of and aggressively hammered to absolute zero within a few short months. By liquidating just 40% of the newly purchased lot, the entire banking debt is completely wiped out. The remaining 60% of unsold inventory instantly transforms into pure, paid-off ammunition. This is the core strength and foundational architecture of Vas & Co. In our theater of operations, inventory is everything. Without inventory, there can be no battles won. Fully paid-off inventory ammunition is the quintessential forte of the fortress."

If I could handle 26% on a credit card to move silk with that level of mathematical precision, a mortgage on a stone building was child's play.

THE CALIFORNIA PIVOT

To a Sovereign, the cost of money is irrelevant as long as the Velocity of the Margin outruns it. I wasn't 'in debt'; I was paying the bank pennies in interest to borrow the fuel that generated thousands in profit. I was leveraging the bank's own greed to fund the extraction of my life from the Montreal slush..." This was the Baptism of Good Debt. I had built a "Slush Fund" of equity that was now melting into Orazon

Gold. The three units in Montreal were no longer just apartments; they were the Liquid Launchpad. The Forge was finally, absolutely complete. I had the cash, the credit, and the internal frequency. I looked at the map of the West Coast. It was time to hunt for the first true P.I.G. .

THE YIELD OF THANKS

(The Gratitude Artery)

I am profoundly grateful for Daniel Martin, the man who eventually looked past the paystub to see the Merchant. I am grateful for 355 Berri, the stone fortress that acted as my shield against the bank's rejection. I am grateful for the 26% Interest, for it was the price of a velocity that the "Robots" will never understand. The Montreal logic has been perfected; the California sun is calling.

VOLUME III: THE ASSET WEAPON

CHAPTER 10: THE DESERT PIVOT

(THE TAILSPIN OF 2011)

10.1 THE DECISIVE SIGNAL: MARTYR OR MAKER?

Fork in the road :

By 2011, my world was vibrating with the frequency of collapse. I had lost both parents to the furnace of time, and my marriage was dissolving under the weight of "Doer vs. Maker" friction. I was the "Good Husband," the one willing to try anything to save the union.

We went to a McGill professor, a marriage counselor with more than thirty diplomas flanking the walls of her office. She was the "Academic Robot's" choice. After a brief audit of our wreckage, the professor looked me in the eye and asked the Devastating Question: “Do you want to be a martyr?”

She meant: *Walk !* . It was the signal. I chose the Sun. I realized that the "Social Clog" of a dying relationship was just another "Printer’s Glitch" holding me back from the Zenith. I chose the Coachella Valley.

10.2 THE GHOST TOWN AUDIT: BAXLEY & THE LANDFILL

I arrived in Indio with a rental car, stripped of my Montreal comforts, carrying nothing but a Merchant’s Eye. I didn't go to the "Plush" saturated markets of Palm Springs to buy a vanity project. I looked for the Glitch.

I met Dick Baxley, a veteran broker of the "Old Guard." To him, Old Town Indio was a landfill for the Great Recession. As we parked on Miles Avenue, the silence was heavy. Every other storefront was a "Wound"—plywood boards and faded "For Lease" signs. Baxley saw a graveyard.

But the Merchant-General sees what is Unfound. I looked at the cracked pavement and I didn't see despair; I saw Low-Velocity Entry. I saw a market where the "Robots" had fled, leaving the coordinates entirely to the Maker.

10.3 THE THREE SOVEREIGN COORDINATES THE P.I.G.s

On a single stretch of Miles Avenue, I positioned my Three Reliable Soldiers. I have changed their identities here to protect their privacy, but their relentless pulse remains the same.

- P.I.G. #1 (Mil1): ELENA (The Retail Artery) — $3,000/mo. Elena brought elegance and a high-frequency bloom to a street that the world had left for dead.

- P.I.G. #2 (Mil2): KURT (The Collector's Vault) — $1,800/mo. Kurt keeps the rhythm of the desert beating through the heat, providing essential value to the seekers.
- P.I.G. #3 (Mil3): MARCO & ROSA (The Craftsmanship Artery) — $2,860/mo. They saw the vision of the "Magic Shop" and turned a ruin into a center of high-quality uncompromising craftsmanship.

TOTAL MONTHLY HONEY: $7,660. While the rest of Indio was hopeless, I was calculating a 28.7% ROI.

10.4 THE ASTRONAUT SURGERY

(MILES AVE)

The "Magic Shop" was the Nucleus. The roof had literally caved in. The city had "Red Tagged" it as a biohazard. I bought the ruin for $83,000—the price of a luxury SUV in 2011.

I watched five men in Astronaut Suits—hazmat gear and oxygen tanks—enter the ruin to decontaminate the soul of the building. Once the "Astronauts" left, I performed a Structural Resurrection. I found tiles for 55 cents in a liquidation section. I spoke Spanish with the craftsmen, building a bond of respect the "Suits" could never understand. Every tile laid was a step away from the martyrdom of the past.

10.5 THE 505 PHILOSOPHY (THE ORAZON SHIELD)

On August 22, 2011, Orazon Inc. was born. I implemented the Real Estate 505 Philosophy:

1. Lower Rent: 20% below market to ensure Zero Vacancy.

2. The $200 Shield: The tenant pays the first $200 of any repair, eliminating "Toilet Calls."

3. The Punctuality Rule: The rent is a "Swiss Clock," paid on the 1st without exception.

I wasn't a "Landlord"; I was a President managing a machine. Because I am on the Donor Side, I do not squeeze my soldiers. By keeping the rent 20% below market, I bought Loyalty.

10.6 THE $5,000,000 ARITHMETIC

- The Acquisition: Total cost for all three units (including the "Astronaut" surgery) was $320,000.
- The Replacement Cost: Rebuilding 6,400 sq. ft. today would cost roughly $2,560,000.

- The Yield Value: At $91,920 annually in a 5% Cap Rate market, the portfolio is worth $1,838,400. When you add the "Heart Premium" of owning the block, your empire stands as a $5,000,000 Shield.

10.7 THE SANARY REALIZATION

I remember the day it clicked in Sanary-Sur-Mer. I looked at my bank portal. The rent had landed. No labor, no trucking, no 40 skids of hosiery to haul. As long as the sun rose over the California desert, I could sit under the sun of the French Riviera. The "Slush" was washed away by the "Milk" of my present. I was no longer a "Doer" chasing a dollar; I was a Sovereign observing a system.

THE YIELD OF THANKS

(THE GRATITUDE ARTERY)

"I am profoundly grateful for the McGill Professor, whose one sentence saved my life. I am grateful for the Astronauts of Indio, who cleaned the air so I could breathe.

I am grateful for the Spanish-speaking craftsmen who knelt with me on the subfloor. They didn't just lay tiles; they healed a wound. I am grateful for Elena, Kurt, and Marco, the healthy bacteria in my fortress.

Finally, I am grateful for the Silence of Sanary, the reward for a lifetime of choosing the Cow over the Mirage. Gratitude is the only investment that returns a 1,000% Yield without ever touching the ledger. BLISS."

CHAPTER 11 [no pun]:

THE CORVETTE VS. THE COW

11.1 THE $100,000 CROSSROADS

THE PALM DESERT AUDIT

In 2019, I stood with my brother, Levon, in the dry heat of Palm Desert. This was the moment of the Great Divergence. I wasn't just showing him a piece of real estate; I was showing him a portal to sovereignty.

I had identified a "Cow"—a clean, premium-grade property for $280,000. The "Milk" yield was a guaranteed $1,500 monthly. Levon had the "Seed": $100,000 sitting in a stagnant bank account, being slowly evaporated by the "Academic Inflation" of the Social Clog.

The Orazon Analysis: I laid out the math on a napkin. A 35% down payment would secure the fortress. The "Small Numbers" of the rent would pay the mortgage, the taxes, and the insurance, leaving a healthy residue of Monthly Honey.

The Academic Fear: Levon hesitated. His eyes were clouded by the Social Fog. He started asking the "Robot Questions": *"What about the HOA fees? What if the taxes go up?"* He was looking at the "Small Problems" and missing the Infinite Horizon. He said the words that are the death knell of the Maker: "I'll think about it."

11.2 THE "I DESERVE IT" PRISON

THE C8 DELUSION

Six months later, the "Thinking" was over. Levon didn't buy the Stone; he bought a C8 Corvette. He walked into the dealership and surrendered his $100,000 to the altar of the Ego. He used the anthem of the middle-class slave: *"I worked hard all my life. I deserve this"*. This is the most dangerous Logical Glitch in the Human Artery. The "Academic" world teaches you that "Hard Work" should be rewarded with "Shiny Objects." The Maker knows that if you work forty years and your reward is a depreciating asset that forces you to work a forty-first year just to pay for its insurance, you haven't "deserved" a reward—you have purchased a Sentence.

11.3 THE STATUS TAX: LACOSTE VS. THE CALCULATION

The "Social Clog" is a vat of manufactured insecurity. It relies on you feeling "incomplete" unless you are draped in the logos of the extraction class. I call this the Status Tax. It is a voluntary levy paid by those who crave the approval of people they don't even like.

I remember the "Doers" in Montreal. They would walk through the grey, biting slush in $110 Lacoste polos. They felt "Elegant." They felt they had "Arrived." But if you looked at their ledger, their arteries were bleeding out. They were paying a

11,000% markup for a piece of cotton with a green crocodile on it.

The Ego Price: 110 Euro.

The Orazon Price: 1 Euro.

Near Sanary, I found the Mirror of Logic. I stood before a liquidation pile at Primark (Ave 83 in La Valette Du Var)—a mountain of high-density, durable cotton shirts reduced from 8 Euro to 1 Euro. These were the same threads, the same mechanical quality, but they lacked the "Ego-Logo." I didn't buy one; I bought the entire frequency. I bought six.

That 109 Euro difference per shirt didn't evaporate. It didn't go to a CEO in Paris to fund his next vanity project. It was Directly Funneled into the Stone. It stayed in the War Chest. When you buy the brand, you are paying for the "Privilege" of being a walking billboard. I am the Hunter of the 1-Euro pile; the "Robot" is the Hunted.

THE FINAL COMMAND: THE PROTOCOL REMAINS

This is the end of the performance. This is where the noise stops and the Sovereign Silence begins. For the Young Vasken who has survived the "Baptism of Slush" and mastered the "Flea Market Math," the path is no longer a mystery. It is a hard-coded directive.

THE PROTOCOL REMAINS:

- Protect the Seed. (Never eat your capital).
- Buy the Cow. (Annex the hard asset).
- Drink the Milk. (Live only on the yield).
- Disappear into the Sanary Silence. (Kill the ego and enjoy the Zenith).

11.4 THE INCOGNITO SHIELD (THE ART OF BEING A GHOST)

The Status Tax has a secondary, more lethal cost: Visibility. When you wear the $110 shirt and drive the $100,000 Corvette, you are broadcasting your "Meaty Artery" to every Vulture in the atmosphere.

The plumber sees the Corvette and doubles the quote. The government sees the Lacoste and sharpens the audit. By choosing the 1-Euro Shield, I achieve the Incognito Protocol. When I walk the docks of Sanary-sur-Mer, I am invisible. I am a ghost. The "Robots" on the 50-meter yachts look at me and see a "Nobody." This is my ultimate luxury. My confidence doesn't come from the fabric on my back; it comes from the $7,660 Artery pumping from a desert 10,000 kilometers away.

11.5 THE ANATOMY OF THE LEAK (MECHANICAL SUICIDE)

The "Robot" looks at a C8 Corvette and sees 490 horsepower. The Maker looks at the same machine and sees a Vacuum of Life Force:

1. Immediate Amputation (Depreciation): The moment the tires touched the asphalt, $20,000 evaporated. That is 2,000 hours of high-density human labor—gone in seconds.
2. The Insurance Ransom: A monthly tribute to protect a "Shiny Object" from the world.
3. The Maintenance Clog: Levon doesn't own the car; the car owns his peace of mind.

11.6 THE MIRROR OF TIME: 2019–2026 AUDIT

THE LEDGER OF TRUTH: THE LEVON PATH VS. THE ORAZON PATH

THE LEVON PATH (Corvette)

Initial Capital: $100,000 (Cash)

Current Value (2026): ~$50,000

Income (The Milk): $0 (Negative Flow)

Operating Costs: $400/mo (Insurance/Gas)

Total Result: -$50,000 in the Red

THE ORAZON PATH (The Cow)

Initial Capital: $100,000 (Down Payment)

Current Value (2026): ~$500,000

Income (The Milk): $126,000 (Total Honey)

Operating Costs: $0 (Tenant Pays Everything)

Total Result: +$526,000 in the Green

The Asymmetric Swing: $576,000. This is the high-definition cost of vanity. For the price of a roaring engine, my brother bought a life of Anxious Maintenance. For the price of a "Fire Ruin" and some 55-cent tiles, I bought Eternal Choice.

11.7 THE OXYGEN MASK AXIOM

In a world of relentless devaluation, Hard Assets are the only way to breathe. Think of the global economy as a high-altitude flight. Inflation is a sudden drop in cabin pressure. When the masks drop, the "Ego Slave"—distracted by his shiny dashboard—realizes too late that his cash is a vacuum.

Only the Maker has access to the oxygen. While the value of the dollar plummets, the value of the Stone and the Milk adjust in real-time. The fortress breathes for you.

11.8 THE CAPITAL TRAP (MEAT VS. MILK)

To the Young Vaskens: Understand the difference between the Meat (your capital) and the Milk (your yield).

Levon ate the Meat. Now, at 70 years old, he is tired and tethered to the "Social Clog." He must continue to work to feed the machine. I protected the Meat and I drank the Milk. My $100,000 stayed in the Stone. It birthed the Monthly Honey that now funds my life in Sanary. I don't need a loud engine to prove I am a General; the Silence of my Bank Account is the only roar I require.

THE YIELD OF THANKS (THE GRATITUDE ARTERY)

I am profoundly grateful for the 1-Euro Polo, the uniform of my liberation. I am grateful for the C8 Corvette, for it serves as the ultimate anatomical study of the 'Status Trap'.

I am grateful for the Silence of Sanary, the reward for a lifetime of choosing the Cow over the Mirage. I am grateful that I am no longer a 'Doer' performing for an audience, but a Maker observing the horizon. BLISS.

CHAPTER 12: THE GILDED NOOSE

(The Primary Residence Audit & The Small Numbers Protocol)

I. THE SOVEREIGN FILTER: COW VS. LEECH

Before you buy a watch, a car, or a kingdom, you must apply the Binary Filter. To the "Academic Robot," an asset is anything you own that has "value." To the Maker, that definition is a lethal trap. In the Orazon Protocol, we do not care about "Estimated Value"; we care about the Direction of the Artery.

AN ASSET (THE COW): A machine that pumps money INTO your pocket while you sleep. If you stopped working today, this machine would keep you alive. (e.g., A rented storefront, a dividend-paying stock, a royalty-producing book).

A LIABILITY (THE LEECH): A machine that sucks money OUT of your pocket every single month. If you stopped working today, this thing would eventually kill you. (e.g., Your car, your credit card, your Netflix subscription, the home you live in, and —most dangerously—your "Dream Home").

The General's Rule: "Value" is a mirage. "Cash Flow" is the only reality. If it doesn't produce "Milk", it's a liability masquerading as a possession.

II. THE PRIMARY RESIDENCE PARASITE

The "Academic" and the "Realtor" are the High Priests of the Clog. They have spent a century convincing you that your home is your "greatest investment". This is a Systemic Lie designed to keep you tethered to the "Printer's" desk.

The Reality Check:

If you live in it, it is not an investment—it is an Expense.

If it requires your "Meat" (labor) to stay alive every month without producing "Milk" (yield), it is a Parasite. You don’t own the house; the bank owns you. You are merely a glorified caretaker paying for the privilege of maintenance.

THE "EQUITY" ILLUSION:

Equity is “Trapped Oxygen.” The Robots tell you that you are "getting rich" because the market value went up. But you cannot eat that value. You cannot spend that value on goat cheese in Sanary. To touch that money, you must either sell the roof over your head (becoming a "Receiver" of a new high-rent market) or borrow against it (creating a new Debt Clog). You are breathing through a straw while the bank owns the tank.

III. THE LETHAL SPREAD (THE $1.3 MILLION SWING)

Let us perform a Cold Audit of two men standing at the same $100,000 crossroads.

The Numbers Verdict:

The gap between being $3,500 in the hole and $1,660 in the black is $5,160 per month. After 120 months (10 Years), the General has $619,200 in pure honey from the spread alone. When you add the tenant's mortgage pay-down and property appreciation on the P.I.G. , the General's net worth swing is $1,300,000 ahead of the Robot. Numbers don't lie . The Robot has a "Nice Kitchen"; the General has Sovereignty.

THE AUDIT:

THE ROBOT (THE GILDED NOOSE) VS. THE GENERAL (THE ORAZON STRIKE)

THE ROBOT

The Move: Buries $100,000 in a "Dream Home" down payment.

Monthly Artery: -$3,500 (Mortgage, Tax, Insurance, HOA).

Sanctuary: Lives in the Liability (Paid with Blood).

Net Position: -$3,500 in the hole.

THE GENERAL

The Move: Buys P.I.G. #3. Keeps $100,000 as a Soldier.

Monthly Artery: +$2,860 (Milk/Income).

Sanctuary: Rents a clean coordinate for -$1,200.

Net Position: +$1,660 in the black.

IV. THE MOBILITY LAW: GUEST OF THE WORLD

The "Robot" is tethered to a coordinate by a 30-year chain. If the market in his city dies, he dies with it.

The Maker is a Guest of the World. The Sovereign Solution: Rent where you live; own what you rent. By renting your sanctuary, you remain Liquid. Your wealth is not in the walls you sleep in; your wealth is in the Artery that connects your Stone to your Ledger. I can move to the Mediterranean tomorrow because my income is Mobile. I don't own the house; I own the income that buys the world.

V. THE SMALL NUMBERS PROTOCOL

The "Academic Robot" waits for a $1,000,000 windfall to change their life. They ignore the "Change" in their pocket while chasing the "Mirage" on the horizon. The Maker realizes that a million dollars is simply a collection of individual dollars that weren't allowed to leak.

THE $1.00 SOLDIER:

In the Orazon Protocol, we don't see a dollar; we see a Seed.

The Robot's View: “It's just $5.00 for a coffee. It’s just $15.00 for a subscription.”

The Maker's View: "That $1.00 is a soldier. If I keep him, he can become $2.50 through the Vas & Co. machine. If I let him leak, I haven't just lost a dollar; I have lost the Infinite Growth that soldier would have produced."

THE LIFE-FORCE CALCULATION:

To distinguish an asset from a liability in your daily life, stop looking at the "Price Tag" and start looking at the Life-Force Exchange.

Calculate your Hourly Yield: If you earn $20/hour, that is your Life-Force Rate.

Audit the Leech: That $600 monthly car payment isn't "$600"—it is 30 hours of your life every single month.

The Verdict: You are trading nearly 4 days of every month just to sit in a depreciating box. Is that car an asset? No. It is Time-Thief.

THE "SMALL NUMBERS" FORTRESS:

By cutting three "Micro-Clogs" that total $300 a month, you aren't "saving pennies." You are reclaiming $3,600 a year. In 10 years, that "Small Number" becomes $36,000—over a third of the way to the $100,000 Palm Desert Seed. The "General" is not born in a boardroom; he is born in the grocery aisle and the utility bill. He is the one who refuses to let a single "Small Number" leak into the Social Clog.

The Orazon Axiom: “If you cannot protect the $1.00, you will never be trusted to command the $1,000,000. The Artery is built one drop at a time.”

THE YIELD OF THANKS

(THE GRATITUDE ARTERY)

I am profoundly grateful for the Spread, the mathematical gap that creates freedom. I am grateful for the $1.00 Soldier, the smallest unit of my empire.

I am grateful for the Renter's Clarity, which allows me to be a Guest of the World rather than a prisoner of a coordinate. I

am grateful for the Small Numbers, for they are the bricks that built my Sanary Zenith. BLISS.

A NOTE ON STRUCTURAL AUTHENTICITY

The Author is a Sovereign and an Architect of the Behavior Matrix, not a clerk of the academy. While this ledger has been forged under blue skies and blue-chip isolation, it has intentionally not been softened by the "Academic Polishing" of the Social Clog.

If you catch a typo or a repetition, congratulations: it simply means your neurological sensors are functioning and you are actually paying attention to the ledger. to the ledger .

Do not act like a blind heir staring at the wrong details. Focus on the math; ignore the slag.

CHAPTER 13: THE 3.5% ESCALATOR

OILING THE MACHINE & RIDING THE FIRE

I. THE ARCHITECTURE OF THE STAIR-STEP

The "Robot" sees a lease as a fixed burden—a static number that sits on a ledger until it is eroded by the "Printers." The Maker sees a lease as a Dynamic Artery. To triple your yield in a decade without adding "Clog" (more units or employees), you do not rely on a single lever; you use the Double-Action Strike.

THE STAIRCASE OF SOVEREIGNTY (THE MILK MULTIPLIER)

To understand the 20-year trajectory of your P.I.G. , stop looking at "formulas" and start looking at the Nudge and the Jump.

1. THE ANNUAL NUDGE (3.5%): Every year, you apply a Systematic 3.5% Increase. This isn't "greed";

it is a hedge against the inflation of the Social Clog. It keeps your Artery clear of the "Devaluation Virus."

2. THE RENEWAL JUMP (31.2%): Every 5 years, when the lease expires, you perform a Market Audit. You don't just "nudge"; you Jump. You bring the rent back to the "Glitch Floor" of the current reality. In our model, this is a one-time 31.2% strike.

II . THE 20-YEAR LEDGER (THE $7,660 STRIKE)

Let's look at the actual "Honey" produced by your Indio Diamond over two decades of consistent execution:

- YEAR 0 (The Extraction): $7,660 (The Starting Milk)
- YEAR 5 (The First Jump): After 5 years of "Nudges" and the first "Jump," your rent hits $11,940.

- YEAR 10 (The Double Jump): You have now annexed more territory. Your rent is $18,610.
- YEAR 15 (The Triple Jump): The Artery is wide open. You are collecting $29,010.
- YEAR 20 (The Sovereign Zenith): The machine is fully matured. Your monthly honey is $45,210.

THE MAINTENANCE NUDGE (3.5%): This is the annual escalator. It is the "Silent Wind" that keeps the Artery from hardening. It is invisible to the tenant—the cost of two cups of coffee a day—but it compounds every year, neutralizing the decay of the currency.

THE SOVEREIGN RE-CALIBRATION (THE JUMP): This is the tactical strike that happens at renewal (every 3 or 5 years). While the 3.5% keeps you moving, the Lump Sum Jump (often 15% to 30%) snaps the rent back to the High-Altitude Reality of the current market.

THE TITAN'S STAIR-STEP (THE SIMPLE MATH)

Here is how you triple your money in 10 years by doing nothing:

STEP 1: THE BASE (YEAR 0) You start with $7,660 in monthly rent. This is your "Floor."

STEP 2: THE NUDGE (THE ANNUAL CLIMB) Every year, the rent goes up by 3.5%. It's a "Small Number"—the price of a couple of coffees. Over 5 years, this small climb adds about $1,400 to your monthly check.

Rent is now: $9,095.

STEP 3: THE STRIKE (THE 5-YEAR JUMP) Every 5 years, the lease expires. You look at the market and "snap" the rent back to reality with a 31% Jump.

Rent now leaps to: $11,900.

STEP 4: THE REPEAT You do it again. Five more years of the "Nudge" followed by one more "Strike."

THE 10-YEAR RESULT: $18,600.

THE TITAN VERDICT:

In 10 years, you went from $7,660 to $18,600.

You didn't buy a second building.

You didn't hire an employee.

You didn't work an extra hour.

You simply allowed the Stair-step to Annex the wealth for you. This is how you outrun the "Printers" while you sleep in Sanary, in total silence .

III. THE INFLATIONARY ANCHOR: RIDING THE FIRE

The "Robot" fears inflation because it eats his savings. The Merchant loves inflation because it provides the heat that drives the value of the Stone into the stratosphere.

Fixed Debt: Your mortgage payment is a Fixed Anchor. In 2026, it is $2,500; in 2041, it is still $2,500. Because the government prints "Discounted Paper" to pay its own debts, your fixed payment becomes mathematically cheaper every year.

Rising Yield: While the debt stays still, the rent is a living organism protected by the Double-Action Strike , the hedge against inflation and the diminishing purchasing power of money .

The Secret Sauce (The Silent Hedge): The rent raises are only the "Cherry on the Pie." While you are receiving this abundant, heavy cash flow, the Stone itself is rising in Total Silence. This appreciation is the solid anchor of the Orazon Protocol.

IV. THE COST OF THE VOID

(THE VACANCY CLOG)

The "Academic" landlord is obsessed with "Market Rent." He spikes the rent by 15% to "optimize" his ledger, ignores the tenant's humanity, and creates a Clog.

THE LETHAL MATH OF THE VACANCY:

1 Month Vacancy: Lose $2,860.

Clean Up/Broker Fees: ~$3,500.

Total Loss: $6,360 [Providing you find a new qualified tenant within just one month !]

To recover $6,360 through a "Market Spike" of $200/month would take 31 months just to break even. This is a mechanical failure. Greed is a Clog; 100% Occupancy is the Artery. We negotiate DOWN to keep the tenant in place, ensuring the "Honey" never stops flowing.

V. THE $200 SHIELD

(THE RESPONSIBILITY COMPONENT)

This is the most important "Oiling" mechanism in the machine. By requiring the tenant to pay the first $200 of any repair, you achieve three Strategic Triumphs :

Elimination of "Toilet Calls": It acts as a biological filter. If a lightbulb flickers, the tenant fixes it. They do not call the General in Sanary for a $20 problem.

Creation of Ownership: Because they have "Skin in the Game," they treat the unit with Proprietary Respect. They don't abuse the HVAC or the plumbing because they are the first line of financial defense.

The Sovereignty of Time: This is the secret to the 30-Minute Work Week. You have built a machine where the parts are self-lubricating. You are granted the Silence of Provence because you have outsourced the "Small Clogs."

VI. PRINCIPAL DIRECTIVE 505: THE WIN-WIN ARBITRAGE

Commercial Rent Generating Real Estate 505

Vasken Der Boghossian

President at ORAZON Inc. a California C-Corp / MBA at Webster University Geneva CH

August 6, 2024

Landrords :

When dealing with mom and pop storefront tenants , more so than with corporate tenants , and while negotiating a lease , negotiate the monthly rent amount down instead of up .. Yes , and i explain . Start by giving factual figures of the going average rent per square foot in the immediate vicinity backed up by the sources of your numbers (LoopNet and Crexi are relaible sources) with local live examples if you can .. Be clear and make it sound as conditional , the importance of paying their rent on the first of each month , and no later that the first .. then tell them you are willing to give them a great deal . Many landlords mistakenly focus on maximizing the dollar volume of the rental income rather than focusing on the stability of a steady flawless inbound cashflow .

Landlords tend to forget they have competition , the landlord next door .

Never think if you overcharge your tenant or ask for the full market price you are benefitting your business in the medium long run .. in fact it is the opposite .. you need to charge 10 to 15% lower than the average market rent price for prime to average locations (even 20% in some cases , for the location vulnerable) . This way you create a win-win situation where you have tenants who value their landlord, who would not look for another property that has better value throughout their lease period which would lead to defaulting their lease and moving out of the premises prematurely . A 15 % lower (than market) price is the equivalent of 2 months' rent . Consider it an investment toward your tenant's loyalty , now you have the upper hand , your tenant would never bother you for pety issues , they would always pay their rent on time , you can rest assured .

Remember , a 3 or 5 year lease is a pretty long commitment , by lowering the rent amount you create a cushion for your tenant , extremely crucial in case of a hiccup and hiccups happen all the time , inevitable during the course of such a lease .

Then to your favor, add a couple of strings to the contract , such as

>> the first $200.- of any repair job on the premises is paid by tenant , each case apart.

>> perhaps add a cap on , say , the water bill , if water is included in the lease , so that consumption of water is minimised and its abuse eliminated ..

>> Raise their security deposit to an amount equivalent to slightly higher than 2 months' rent .

And since your tenant is getting a great deal on the monthly rent amount , they will easily agree on these clauses , which ultimately will help you , the landlord , a lot .

Remember , if it's not a good deal for both parties , it's not good business .

So , by motivating your tenant , you are contributing to the success of your tenant , Their success is your success . Also, you are avoiding defaults hence saving yourself a ton of money spent on lawyers , [btw, who usually take their sweet time to resolve any issue since the longer it drags the more they extort you ! afterall, in the lawyers' mind , landlords are just that "landlords" , and they will write any and every expense off anyway , right ? .. but that's another chapter altogether ..]

So , when you give your tenant a good deal , it comes back to you in tenfold saving time and senseless frustration .. you're buying yourself peace of mind with steady and timely rent income that you can count on every 1st of the month , stabilizing your inbound cashflow .

The main purpose of collecting rent is to protect the property and to have a constant budget for its upkeep and maintenance . Any upgrade to the facilities and aesthetic enhancement will certainly add value to your property and while spending on upgrades is an investment in itself, the amounts spent are tax deductible .. in the meantime the value of your property is going up by the calendar day .

I think I gave away a tad too much, but I hope someone benefits from this and one day will buy me an espresso . I speak from personal extensive experience in this field .

Vasken Der Boghossian President at Orazon Inc . a California C-Corp

VI. THE SOVEREIGN MANIFESTO

(DIRECTIVE 505)

From the Office of the President, ORAZON Inc.

THE MANDATE: When dealing with "Mom and Pop" storefronts, negotiate the monthly rent DOWN. Charge 10% to 15% lower than the average market rent (backed by LoopNet/Crexi data).

THE LOGIC: Maximizing dollar volume is a "Robot's" mistake. Maximizing the Stability of Cashflow is a "Titan's" victory. A 15% lower rent is an investment in Tenant Loyalty. It gives them the cushion to survive the inevitable hiccups of the tenant's business. If they thrive, you thrive.

THE STRINGS (THE PROTECTION):

- The $200 Repair Clause: Outsourcing the "Small Clogs".

- The Water Consumption Cap: Eliminating resource abuse.
- The 2-Month Security Deposit: Strengthening the "Financial Shield".

THE VERDICT: If it’s not a good deal for both parties, it’s not good business. Contributing to your tenant's success is the only way to ensure your own Sovereign Silence.

THE CODIFIED BLUEPRINT: THE STABILO LINES

- "Greed is a Clog; Consistency is an Artery."
- "The 3.5% Escalator is a 'Nudge' that buys you 100% Peace."
- "A vacant unit is a wound; a long-term tenant is a Fortress."
- "The $200 Shield is the wall between your Silence and their Noise."

CHAPTER 14: THE SHINY OBJECT LAW & THE METABOLIC BODY

THE ARCHITECTURE OF GUILT-FREE LUXURY

I. THE BIOLOGICAL RED TAG: THE DECONTAMINATION

In 2011, as I stood on the curb of Miles Avenue watching the "Astronauts" scrub toxic spores from the soul of Miles Avenue, I had a Devastating Realization. I was standing there 20 pounds overweight, inflamed by the "Social Clog" of the Montreal diet, and distracted by the "Noise" of the Ego. I was decontaminating the Stone, but I was still a victim of a Biological Red Tag.

The "Academic Robot" believes health is about "Adding"—more supplements, more superfoods, more expensive bio-hacks. The Maker knows that health, like wealth, is about Extraction. To find the Diamond, you must remove the Dirt. To find the General, you must liquidate the Fat. You cannot command a high-frequency empire from a low-frequency engine.

THE ORAZON LAW OF BIOLOGY:

"If your blood is sludge, your decisions will be fog. A body in a state of chronic inflammation is a factory with a clogged exhaust—it will eventually seize, no matter how much gold is in the vault."

II. THE SHINY OBJECT LAW (MEAT VS. MILK)

The "Academic Robot" works for thirty years, saves his "Paper," and then performs a Financial Amputation on his own net worth. He takes $100,000 of Liquid Seed and exchanges it for a machine that loses $20,000 the moment the tires touch the street. This is the Cowardice of Consumption. He used his Meat (capital) to buy a Parasite (the car).

THE SOVEREIGN RULE OF PROCUREMENT:

"You do not buy the Ferrari with your own blood; you buy the Cow (The P.I.G.) first, and let the Milk (The Rent) buy the Ferrari." This is the law that separates the General from the Ego Slave. The Slave uses his time and his blood to pay for a status symbol. The General uses his Method to build an Artery, then uses the "Spillage" of that artery to live as a Guest of his own success.

THE MOVE: THE ROBOT (EGO SLAVE) VS. THE GENERAL (MAKER)

THE ROBOT

The Action: Spends $250,000 cash on a supercar.

The Yield: -$100,000 loss (Depreciation).

The Maintenance: Paid with 2,000 hours of labor.

The Verdict: He ate the Meat.

THE GENERAL

The Action: Invests $250,000 into P.I.G. #4.

The Yield: +$210,000 (5-year Cash Yield).

The Maintenance: Paid by the "Milk" of P.I.G. #4.

The Verdict: The P.I.G. fed him the Ferrari for free.

III. THE INCOGNITO SHIELD: THE 1-EURO PROTOCOL

The Young Vasken must master the art of being a Sovereign Ghost. When I walk the docks of Sanary-sur-Mer, I do not wear the $110 Lacoste "Uniform of the Slave." I wear a high-density, durable 1-Euro cotton polo found in a liquidation pile at Primark (Ave 83 in La Valette Du Var).

- The Vulture Tax: When you broadcast wealth through logos (Lacoste, Rolex), you invite Social Extraction. The plumber sees the

Corvette and doubles the quote. The taxman sees the logo and sharpens the audit.

- The Frequency of Silence: When your bank account is roaring with $7,660 every month, you don't need a green crocodile on your chest to feel like a General. Your confidence comes from the Ledger, not the Label. The 1-Euro Polo is the ultimate armor; it allows you to observe the world without being hunted by it.

IV. THE METABOLIC BODY (OMAD & CELLULAR SURGERY)

The "Food Robots" want you to eat six times a day to keep your insulin spiked. A man on a sugar rollercoaster is reactive, impulsive, and easy to manage. I implemented OMAD (One Meal A Day) to reclaim my biological sovereignty.

THE 23-HOUR SILENCE & THE GHRELIN WAVE:

Hunger is not a "Crisis"; it is a Hormonal Alarm. When the alarm rings, the Robot runs to the fridge. The General acknowledges the noise and remains at his station. After 20 minutes, the Ghrelin Wave passes, the hunger evaporates, and the Laser Focus returns. The brain switches to its On-Board Fuel Tank (Ketones).

CELLULAR SURGERY: THE SEARCH & DESTROY MODE

The most powerful repair crew in the universe is Autophagy :"Self-Eating". By doing Nothing, you trigger an internal metabolic cleansing. After 18 hours of fasting, your system activates "Search & Destroy" mode. It is the biological equivalent of the "Astronaut Suits" entering the ruin to strip the rot.

THE BIOLOGICAL FORGE: THE OMAD STAGES

STAGE 1: 12–16 HOURS

The Action: Insulin Drops.

The Biological Reset : Clearing the "Social Clog".

This is the initial purge. As insulin levels recede, the biological artery is cleared of the noise and inflammation of the external world. The system stops processing external fuel and prepares for the deep internal work.

STAGE 2: 18–24 HOURS

The Action: Autophagy Peaks.

The Cellular Deployment : The "Astronaut Suits" Entering the Ruin.

This is the elite strike. Autophagy—the body's self-cleaning mechanism—reaches its zenith. Imagine a team in pressurized "Astronaut Suits" entering the cellular ruins. They identify damaged proteins and broken structures that have been clogging the machine for years.

THE RESULT

The Action: Recycling Old Cells.

The Metabolic Alchemy : Turning "Trash" into "Bricks".

The forge does not waste. It dismantles the cellular debris identified by the cleaning crew and recycles it into high-quality building materials. You are not merely fasting; you are dismantling the weak versions of yourself to manufacture the bricks for your new foundation.

V. THE FINAL AUDIT:

LIQUIDATING THE 20-POUND LIABILITY

I didn't just "lose weight." I Liquidated a 20-Pound Liability. Those 20 pounds were the "Primary Residence" of my biology—they required "Insurance" (medication), produced "Clogs" (fatigue), and yielded Zero Milk. By stripping that weight through the Jamnadas Mandate, I increased my Physical and Mental Velocity

THE YIELD OF THANKS: DR. PRADIP JAMNADAS

I sit in Sanary today, 20 pounds lighter and infinitely sharper, because I stopped listening to the "Food Robots" and started listening to the High-Frequency Wisdom of Dr. Pradip Jamnadas.

To Dr. Jamnadas: My nutrition idol and mentor. Thank you for the courage to speak the "Bitter Truth". You taught me that hunger is not a problem to be solved, but a Weapon to be wielded. My "Engine" is now as clean as the 55-cent tiles on Miles Avenue.

THE CODIFIED BLUEPRINT: STABILO LINES

- "The body is the Primary Asset; if the heart is a Clog, the empire is a ruin."

- "Hunger is the Quenching Process of the spirit."
- "Own the Cow, rent the Ferrari."
- "The 1-Euro Polo is the ultimate armor; visibility is a tax."

CHAPTER 15 THE INCOGNITO PROTOCOL

SUBTITLE: THE TACTICAL INVISIBILITY OF THE SOVEREIGN GHOST

I. THE GEOGRAPHY OF THE WIN: LIQUIDATING "WORK"

The "Social Clog" teaches you to work for a "Vacation." You are programmed to suffer for fifty weeks in a grey office so you can spend two weeks in a crowded hotel—essentially paying the "Printers" for a temporary permission slip to breathe.

The Maker rejects this extraction. I didn't want a "Break" from my life; I wanted a New Life where the concept of "Work" was liquidated. I chose Sanary-sur-Mer. Not because it was "Expensive"—the metric of the Robot—but because it was Crystalline. In Sanary, the rhythm is dictated by the sun and the Mediterranean wind, not by the "Academic Clock."

Here, time is not a resource to be sold; it is a territory to be occupied.

II. THE RADAR OF THE VULTURE (VISIBILITY IS A LIABILITY)

THE STATUS TAX

The "Academic" believes that success must be signaled. They seek the "Gold Star" and the loudest table at the restaurant, unaware that Visibility is a Liability. When the world sees your "Big Numbers," the world sharpens its teeth. The tax man, the jealous neighbor, and the "Social Vultures" are all drawn to the scent of exposed meat.

THE 1-EURO POLO SHIELD

The Sovereign Merchant operates on a Parallel Frequency. In Sanary, my greatest tactical advantage is my Anonymity. I walk the docks in a 1-Euro Polo from a liquidation bin (Primark Ave 83). I am the man buying the dorade directly from the fisherman's wood, not the one shouting from the deck of a 50-meter yacht.

The Glitch of Perception: The "Robots" equate wealth with flash. By removing the flash, you remove the target from your back.

The Sovereign Shield: Being Incognito allows you to observe the market without the market observing you. You see the "Glitches" because you aren't distracted by your own reflection.

III. THE ARITHMETIC OF SELF-SATISFACTION

The most dangerous "Clog" is the need for others to acknowledge your success. If your satisfaction requires an audience, you are a Slave to the Mirror. True achievement is a private conversation between you and your Ledger.

"When the 3 P.I.G.s are oiling themselves and the 'Monthly Honey' lands in silence, you don't need a 'Like' or a 'Follow' to feel the weight of your victory. The silence is the proof of the quality."

THE FREQUENCY FORMULA

We define the Sovereign Frequency as a simple balance sheet: your Internal Assets divided by your need for External Proof.

Look at the mechanics of the ledger. If a man has $100,000 in hidden assets but wastes $100,000 on luxury cars and watches to prove his status, his frequency is low—he is net zero, trapped in the social fog. But when your need for External Proof drops to a flat zero, the math changes completely. The moment you stop wasting your metal to show the world that you are winning, your real power becomes mathematically limitless. The Ghost has no need to signal; the Ghost simply accumulates.

The less you have to prove, the more you actually Are.

IV. THE "NOURRI, LOGÉ, BLANCHI" FORMULA (GLOBAL ARBITRAGE)

In Sanary, I am "Nourri, Logé, Blanchi"—Fed, Lodged, and Laundered—by the foresight of 2011. The math of the Zenith is a masterclass in Proprietary Arbitrage :

Component, Financial Value

The Input (California P.I.G.s), Strong US Dollars

The Output (Sanary Lifestyle), Euros

Monthly Honey $7,660

Total Expenditure, less than $2,500

Every month, the 3 P.I.G.s produce a massive surplus. I spend what I need on the best goat cheese and fresh fish. The "Residue" goes back into the War Chest. I am not "spending" my wealth; I am Living on the Spillage. Meanwhile, my net worth continues its unyielding march toward the North Star.

V. THE 30-MINUTE OILING MANUAL (THE OVERSEER PROTOCOL)

The "Social Clog" tells you that an empire requires a 40-hour grind. This is a Mechanical Lie. If your P.I.G.s are healthy, you are no longer a "Worker"—you are an Overseer. Once a month, I perform the Standard Audit:

The Artery Check: Verify the "Honey" has landed from Elena , Kurt , Marco and Rosa .

The Health Check: Review "Maintenance Pings." (Filtered by the $200 Shield Rule).

The Small Numbers: Ensure no "Leeches" have attached themselves to the Artery.

The Result: Total management time is 30 Minutes. The remaining 43,170 minutes of the month are Pure Sovereignty.

VI. THE METRIC OF THE BLANK LEDGER

The ultimate metric of wealth is not how much you have, but how much you don't have to do.

The Slave Metric: A day full of "High-Value" meetings and urgent calls.

The Maker Metric: A day that begins with a Blank Ledger.

If you are "Busy", you are failing the Protocol. Being busy is a sign of a "Clog" in your management system. The Orazon Zenith is achieved when your presence is no longer required for your prosperity. You are the Sovereign Ghost moving silently through the sun, while your assets oil themselves 10,000 kilometers away.

VII. THE BROTHER'S MIRROR (CORVETTE VS. COW)

I look at my brother, Levon, not with judgment, but as a Warning Light. He chose the Ego Slave path: a C8 Corvette that bleeds his artery into a machine.

The Reflection: He polishes his dashboard to feel alive; I polish my Ledger of Thanks to stay free.

The Reality: The $7,660 that lands from California every month allows me to be a Propeller of Goodness, while he remains a victim of maintenance.

The Lesson: I am grateful for the "Toilet Calls" he feared, for those clogs were the gatekeepers of the kingdom. Because he wouldn't clear the pipes, I now own the ocean.

VIII. THE UNIVERSAL LEDGER

(THE KARMA FEEDBACK LOOP)

If religion is the "Printed Lie" used to control the weak, then Karma is the "Original Code" used to balance the universe. It is Systemic Feedback.

The Unexpected Reward (The Donor Yield): When you act from the Donor Side—helping a "Young Vasken" or clearing a "Clog" with zero expectation of return—you are depositing Residual Honey into a hidden vault. It arrives as an Unexpected Strike: a "Sardine Key" that opens a door in Portugal you didn't even know existed.

The "Ass-Bite" (The Structural Leak): When you poison an Artery for a "Big Number" shortcut, you create a Debt. The Universal Ledger always collects. It bites your ass when you least expect it—usually when you think your fortress is finished.

THE LAW: "A clean Ledger is the only way to sleep in the Sanary Sun. If your Artery is built on 'Rotten Meat,' the smell will eventually draw the Vultures."

IX. STABILO LINES

“Never Signal: The 1-Euro polo is your armor.”

“Decouple the Coordinate: Earn in USD; spend in Provence.”

“Invisibility is the ultimate armor; Silence is the ultimate luxury.”

“Achievement is not 'Making it'; it is the freedom to NOT have to prove you made it.”

“If you can walk through a crowd of Vultures and remain invisible, you have won the game.”

X. THE YIELD OF THANKS

THE SOURCE

The "Robot" seeks the light. The Sovereign Ghost has realized that He Is the Source. I sit at a café in Sanary and feel a deep, Anchored Yield of Gratitude.

I am grateful for the Fire at Bob’s Magic Shop, for without the ruin, there would be no Diamond. I am grateful for the Montreal Burn, for without the fire, there would be no wings. I am grateful for the 3 P.I.G.s, for they are the silent soldiers that stand guard over my peace.

CHAPTER 16

THE ORAZON CREED

THE CONSTITUTION OF THE MAKER

I. THE INHERITANCE OF LOGIC:

THE PASSING OF THE CANE

The "Academic" believes that inheritance is about "Giving Money". They hand over a check to a "Receiver" who has never felt the heat of the Forge, and they wonder why the wealth evaporates into the Social Clog within a decade. Giving money to an unconditioned mind is like pouring high-octane fuel into a rusted engine—it only accelerates the breakdown.

The Maker knows that true inheritance is the Software of Sovereignty. I am not just leaving an estate; I am leaving you the Cane of 1915—the Absolute Ability to see the "Glitch" in the machine.

This is the Inheritance of Logic.

To the next generation of our bloodline, and to all Young Vaskens seeking sovereignty across the global artery: If you follow these Five Iron Gates, you will walk through the furnace of any century."

II. THE FIVE IRON GATES

GATE 1: MAINTAIN THE CLEAN ARTERY (Biological Sovereignty)

"If you cannot control the fork, you cannot control the fortune". You cannot build a fortress on a swamp. If you cannot control your insulin, you cannot control your interest rates. The Maker knows they are the same Artery.

The Mandate: Master the OMAD (One Meal A Day) frequency. Trigger Autophagy daily.

The Logic: At the 14th hour of the fast, the "Academic Fog" lifts and your mind becomes a Piercing Laser. Your body begins to consume its own Cellular Waste, cleaning the pipes for high-frequency thought.

The Standard: A clean intestine is the foundation of a clean ledger. Liquidate the Fat—it is a biological debt that produces Zero Milk.

GATE 2: MOVE FROM RECEIVER TO PRINTER

(The Identity Shift)

"Authority is just ink on a page. Be the one holding the pen." The world is designed to make you a Receiver. Schools want "Doers" who wait for the bell. The system trains you to be the Paper—passive and printed upon.

The Mandate: Perform a Ruthless Unlearning of the "Printed Lie".

The Logic: The Printer is the one who creates the terms, signs the checks, and designs the assets. You do not ask for value; you Print it.

The Standard: Never ask for a "Permission Slip" to exist. Identify the Glitch in the market, strike with High-Density Words, and print your own reality.

GATE 3: HONOR THE GEOMETRIC MULTIPLIER

(The Financial Formula)

"The Robot counts his salary; the General counts his Markup." Never trade your time for a "Linear" salary that is taxed at the source. Linear gains are the "Crumbs" of the slave; geometric gains are the "Milk" of the General.

The Mandate: Follow the $1.00 to $2.50 Alchemy established in the Silk Multiplier. Seek Margins, not Volume.

The Logic: Small Numbers feed the P.I.G.s. If you buy for $1.00 and sell for $2.50, your cost is recovered at 40% sales. The remaining 60% is Infinite Gold.

The Standard: Aim for the 28.7% ROI. If the deal doesn't result in a P.I.G. that pays for itself in 3.5 years, it is a "Clog."

GATE 4: BUILD THE ASSET SHIELD

(The Sovereignty Buffer)

"Own the Stone, rent the Sanctuary". A paycheck is a temporary high; an Asset is a permanent fortress. Your primary residence is a Parasite; your car is an Ego-Leech.

The Mandate: Follow the Shiny Object Law. Own the Stone, rent the Sanctuary.

The Logic: Never buy the Ferrari with your own blood; buy the Cow first, and let the Milk buy the luxury. Leverage is a Propeller when used for Good Debt and a Noose when used for Bad Debt.

The Standard: Redundancy ensures survival. One unit is a risk; three units is a Fortress. Stay Liquid, stay Mobile, stay Incognito.

GATE 5: ACHIEVE THE SANARY SILENCE

(The Ultimate Metric)

"Wealth is not what you spend; it is the time you own".

The final goal is not "Wealth"; it is Silence.

The Mandate: Aim for the 30-Minute Work Week. Implement the $200 Shield and the 3.5% Escalator to build a machine that oils itself.

The Logic: True success is not being the "loudest" in the room; it is being the Sovereign Ghost the room doesn't even know is there.

The Standard: Wear the 1-Euro Polo—it is the armor of the Free. The greatest luxury is the Silence of an obligation-free morning.

III. THE ORAZON OATH

"I will not be digested by the State. I will not be distracted by the Shiny Object. I will protect the Artery with Surgical Precision. I will remain a Ghost to the Vultures and a Source to my People".

IV. STABILO LINES: THE LEGACY FILTER

"The 1915 Furnace burned the wood; it only hardened the Porcelain".

The P.I.G. is a living organism; respect its health, and it will give you its Milk.

"Sovereignty is the transition from 'Seeking the Light' to 'Being the Source' ".

"If you can walk through a crowd of Vultures and remain invisible, you have won the game".

"Wealth is not what you spend; it is the time you own".

VOLUME V:

THE ZENITH

CHAPTER 17:

THE SANARY ZENITH

THE DEATH OF THE EGO

AND THE 100-YEAR LEGACY

I. THE MEDITERRANEAN MIRROR:

THE 8:15 AM RITUAL

The "Robot" believes that the finish line is a "Big Number." They spend forty years sprinting toward a pile of gold, only to find that their Ego has grown faster than their bank account. They buy a 50-meter yacht—not for the ocean, but for the audience. They have traded a grey office for a white boat, but they remain "Receivers" of external validation. In Sanary-sur-Mer, the light is different. It is a Liberating Light. At 8:15 AM, as the Provençal sun hits the harbor, the world is stripped of its illusions.

I perform the morning audit: I look at my calendar. It is empty. I look at my phone. It is silent. The Achievement: True wealth is not measured in what you own, but in what you don't have to do. This is the Zenith—the transition from selling your time as a currency to occupying it as a territory. If you have nothing to do, you have reached the level of a Maker. You have bought back your life force from the "Printers".

II. THE SUICIDE OF THE STATUS EGO

The most difficult extraction was never the money from the banks; it was the Ego from the soul. The "Status Ego" is a parasite that lives on the "Likes" of the "Social Clog." To enter the Zenith, you must murder that version of yourself.

THE GHOST RATIO

Sovereignty is the distance between your Wealth and your Signal. To become a Sovereign Ghost, you must increase your "Milk" while decreasing your "Signal." A true Titan has a massive ledger but looks like a "Nobody" on the docks of Sanary. We define the Sovereign Frequency as your Internal Assets divided by your External Proof. The Slave Scenario: If you have $100,000 in assets but spend $100,000 on a car to show off, your frequency is 1. You are visible. You are a target. The General Scenario: If you have $10,000,000 in assets but wear a 1-Euro Polo and stay invisible, your frequency approaches infinity. You are weightless.

III. THE GEOGRAPHY OF BLISS: GLOBAL ARBITRAGE

In the "Octagon", you buy processed products from a shelf. In the Zenith, you buy Life from the Source. I buy the dorade royal directly from the fisherman's wooden boat (pointus), still smelling of the

Mediterranean salt. This is High-Frequency Nutrition.

THE NOURRI, LOGÉ, BLANCHI FORMULA

I am "Fed, Lodged, and Cleaned" by the foresight of the 2011 strike.

Component Strategic Asset Strategy :

The Input (USD) : 3 P.I.G.s (California) generating $7,660 Monthly Honey.

The Output (EUR) : less than $2,500 Total Sanary Expenses.

The Zenith Result : A Surplus Fortress continuously appreciating in value

IV. THE OVERSEER PROTOCOL:

THE 30-MINUTE OILING MANUAL

If your P.I.G.s are healthy, you are no longer a "Worker"—you are an Overseer. Once a month, I perform the Standard Audit: The Artery Check: Verify the "Honey" has landed from the primary asset distribution channels. The Health Check: Review "Maintenance Pings" (Filtered by the $200 Shield Rule). The Small Numbers: Ensure no "Leeches" have attached themselves to the Artery. The Result: Total management time is 30 Minutes. The remaining 43,170 minutes of the month are Pure Sovereignty.

V. THE CENTURY ARCHITECT: THE 100-YEAR AUDIT

The Multigenerational Timeline

Year 2026 (The Zenith):

Monthly Honey: $7,660

Annual Artery: $91,920

Year 2050 (The First Hand-off):

Monthly Honey: $18,735

Annual Artery: $224,820

Year 2126 (The Century Mark):

Monthly Honey: $238,405

Annual Artery: $2,860,860

By 2126, a single storefront in Indio will produce more in a single month than a "High-Earning Robot" makes in an entire year today. And beneath that compounding income engine lies the ultimate asymmetry: while the Robot trades finite hours. for a diminishing paycheck, the underlying value of the assets ascends to meet the sky. This is why we buy the Stone.

VI. THE SUCCESSOR'S TEST: THE THREE FILTERS

To prevent the "Heir of the Ego Slave" from liquidating the fortress, the hand-off is governed by Three Ironclad Filters: The Biological Audit: Does the successor master the OMAD frequency? If they cannot control their fork, they cannot control a

Diamond. The Flea Market Forge: Every successor must spend one year in the trenches. They must feel the "Dirt" of the Markup before they touch the "Honey" of the Rent. The 1-Euro Shield: They must walk through a high-status room in a 1-Euro polo. If they require a logo to feel powerful, they are a Vulture-in-waiting.

VII. THE KARMA LEDGER: UNIVERSAL ACCOUNTABILITY

THE LAWS OF THE UNIVERSAL LEDGER

Karma is the Original Code—the infallible feedback loop of the universe.

The Unexpected Reward: When you act from the Donor Side with zero expectation of return, you deposit Residual Honey into a hidden vault. It arrives as an Unexpected Strike.

The "Ass-Bite": When you hurt the vulnerable for a

shortcut, you create a Debt. The Universal Ledger always collects.

The Law: A clean Ledger is the only way to sleep in the Sanary Sun. If your Artery is built on "Rotten Meat," the smell will eventually draw the Vultures. Unexpected Strike.

VIII. THE BROTHER'S MIRROR (CORVETTE VS. COW)

I look at my brother, Levon, as a Warning Light. He chose the Ego Slave path: a C8 Corvette that bleeds his artery into a machine. He polishes his dashboard to feel alive; I polish my Ledger of Thanks to stay free. The $7,660 that lands from California every month allows me to be a Propeller of Goodness, while he remains a victim of maintenance. I am grateful for the "Toilet Calls" he feared—those clogs were the gatekeepers of the kingdom. Because he wouldn't clear the pipes, I now own the ocean.

X. THE YIELD OF THANKS

I sit at a café in Sanary, watching the "Robots" rush by. I feel a deep, unassailable Yield of Gratitude.

I am grateful for the Fire at Bob's Magic Shop, for without the ruin, there would be no Diamond.

I am grateful for the Montreal Burn, for without the fire, there would be no wings.

I am grateful for the 3 P.I.G.s, for they are the silent soldiers that stand guard over my peace.
I am Vasken. I am the General. I have outsmarted the borders, the banks, and my own Ego.

And the view from the Zenith is Absolute. STABILO LINES : "True wealth is the freedom to NOT have to prove you made it". "If your presence is required for your prosperity, you are not a Maker; you are a high-paid Slave". "Invisibility is the ultimate armor; Silence is the ultimate luxury".

CHAPTER 18: THE ORAZON AUDIT

SUBTITLE: THE 20-YEAR GLITCH & THE $50M VERDICT

I. THE VISION: SEEING THE INVISIBLE

THE PIGEON-DROPPING PROPHET

Young Vasken, listen closely. To the "Robot" trapped in the Academic Fog, the world is just a series of jobs and bills. But to the General, the world is a map of Arteries. In 2002, I was standing in the grease and grit of the Old Port of Montreal flea market. While the "Robots" were browsing for junk under the constant bombardment of pigeons from the rusted beams above, I was performing a Strategic Audit of the future. I saw a Glitch so massive it could swallow the planet. I saw the collision of the two most powerful forces in human history: Logic and Distribution. I realized that if a man could own the bridge between the "Brain" of the digital age and the "Body" of global shipping, he would own the Zenith.

THE ORAZON EQUATION (ORA + ZON)

I didn't pick a name only because it "sounded good". I performed a Strategic Fusion Fusion of the two "Printers of the Century":

ORA (Oracle): Larry Ellison's kingdom. This is the Logic. It is the database—the "Stone" of the digital age that holds the records of every human transaction.

ZON (Amazon): Jeff Bezos's empire. This is the Distribution. It is the global pipe, the Escalator that moves the "Honey" from the factory floor to the front door. I fused them. I birthed ORAZON. I annexed the digital real estate immediately, securing orazon.com over 20 years ago. While the "Robots" were buying toys, I was holding the keys to the Master Artery. This was my first Digital Stone—no mortgage, no tax bill, just pure Sovereign Potential.

II. THE "AMACLE" GLITCH:
TOOLS VS. MACHINES
THE $4,888 TRAP

The Clean Blueprint

Look at how lethal this sequence reads when you drop the upgrade in and let it flow into the next line:

You might ask: "General, what about the other side? Why didn't you book AMACLE.com?" Today, some speculator has listed it for $4,888 USD as a "Premium Domain". I look at that price and I laugh.

Why? Because the General does not buy Tools; the General builds Engines.

The Tool: A domain name is just a hammer. A hammer is worth $20.

The Engine: A Money Machine built with that hammer is worth $50 Million.

The "Robots" are flipping domains for a few

thousand dollars—the "Small Slush". I am building Enduring Arteries. I chose ORAZON as the Genetic Code for a multi-million dollar empire. Let the speculators keep their $4,888 "tools". I'll keep my $50,000,000 machine.

III. THE TRINITY OF STONES: THE 3 P.I.G.sTHE INDIO FORTRESS

My kingdom was built on the Stone. I didn't buy "Paper Dreams"; I bought the Artery of Indio. On August 22, 2011, I legally sealed the logic by registering ORAZON Inc. in California [C Corp #3407268]. This fortress houses the biological reality of the 111-Day Burn: P.I.G. 1 & 2 (The Twins): X1 & X2 Miles Ave. Two high-density units in the heart of Old Town Indio. P.I.G. 3 (The Anchor): X3 Miles Ave. The third unit, completing the Indio fortress. Together, these are the 3 P.I.G.s—the physical proof that the Orazon Protocol is not a theory, but a Physical Reality.

IV. THE ICARUS BLINDNESS:

THE TRIPLE STRIKE

THE TEST OF THE EMPERORS

In April and May 2024, I decided to test the "Emperors." I issued an Incisive Strike to the three men who claim to own the future: Jeff Bezos, Larry Ellison, and Elon Musk. My strategy was Sovereign Leverage. I offered the "Bridge" [ORAZON.com], the "Fortress" [ORAZON Inc.], and the 3 P.I.G.s to each of them for a total of $10 Million. I wanted to see if their "Decency" matched their "Data".

But the Blind Icari flew too close to the Sun of their own trillions. They have so many "Assistants" and "Vultures" guarding their gates that a direct strike from a Maker is treated as "Noise".

They missed the Architectural DNA of the next century.

V. THE SMOKING GUNS: THE EVIDENCE

STRIKE 1 — THE DISTRIBUTION EMPEROR

FROM: vasken@vasken.com | TO: jeff@amazon.com DATE: April 2, 2024 (Re-sent May 2, 2024) SUBJECT: ORAZON TEXT: "Hi Jeff, i hope you are very well. i am the owner of ORAZON Inc, a California C-Corp that exists since 2011. i am also the owner of www.orazon.com which is parked and inactive. Orazon owns 2 commercial properties in Indio, California... i am willing to sell Orazon Inc and Orazon.com... Thanks and regards, Vasken Der Boghossian."

RESULT: DEAFENING SILENCE.

STRIKE 2 – THE LOGIC KING

FROM: vasken@vasken.com | TO: larry.ellison@oracle.com DATE: April 8, 2024 (Re-sent May 2, 2024) SUBJECT: ORAZON TEXT: "hi Larry, i hope you are very well... i am willing to sell Orazon Inc and Orazon.com. Please let me know if you would be interested in acquiring them... Thanks and regards, Vasken Der Boghossian."

RESULT: DEAFENING SILENCE.

STRIKE 3 – THE ENERGY ARCHITECTFROM: vasken@vasken.com | TO: elon@spacex.com / elon@tesla.com DATE: April 8, 2024 (Re-sent May 2, 2024) SUBJECT: ORAZON TEXT: "attn Elon Musk, hi Elon, i hope you are very well... i am willing to sell Orazon Inc and Orazon.com... Thanks and regards, Vasken Der Boghossian."

RESULT: DEAFENING SILENCE.

VI. THE MASTER MARKUP:

THE $50M VERDICT

THE REVALUATION STRIKE

Their silence was the greatest Intrinsic Gift I ever received. While they let these emails rot, I birthed the 4th P.I.G.—this book. The "Grace Period" is over. Because the package now includes the Algorithm of Sovereignty, the price has quintupled. THE NEW VALUATION $ 50,000,000 Gross + 10% Royalty .

NOTE TO THE VULTURES:

This 10% royalty is on Gross Sales. I do not play the "Net Profit" game where accountants hide the honey behind tax-deductible debris. Every book sold feeds the ORAZON Artery at the top line.

VII. THE POWER OF SMALL NUMBERS

THE $1.50 SEED

Young Vasken, you might read this and think $50,000,000 is a "Big Number." You might not be impressed by a man standing in a dusty flea market, converting 1 Canadian Dollar into 2.50. But that is where you fail. The $50 million isn't a miracle; it is the Multiplied Echo of that first $1.50 profit. If you cannot master the "Small Numbers" with discipline and gratitude, you will never touch the "Big Dough." Never underestimate the seed, or you will never own the forest.

THE MARGIN OF THE SOVEREIGN MAKER

Look closely at the numbers, for they trace the true trajectory of a lifetime. Decades ago, as a student in Switzerland, I nourished myself on 1 CHF tins of sardines while my peers chased social mirages over

25 CHF restaurant meals—quietly capturing a 24 CHF daily spread that laid my first mental foundations. Today, the Merchant General still hunts the exact same glitches, only the spreads have grown wider. A simple 1 Euro polo covers the skin just as well as a 120 Euro Lacoste shirt bought by an insecure robot to impress a society that doesn't care —leaving a 119 Euro spread safely inside my perimeter. A 20-centime home-brewed Lavazza espresso tastes far more robust and gratifying than the 2 Euro cup at the corner café, securing a 1.80 Euro margin on a basic daily ritual.

The domesticated mind mocks these tiny amounts, completely blind to the mathematical reality of aggregation. Over time, these daily spreads compound into an unshakeable stack of pure, raw capital—the exact capital required to secure the downpayment on a cash-flowing rental property. This downpayment is the first wall that 99% of the population can never climb. They look at property owners and complain about a systemic shortage of funds, but the truth is far more damning: they are bleeding to death from controllable addictions and social vices, trading their ultimate freedom for overpriced coffee and corporate labels. Every single dollar, euro, or franc you mindlessly hand over to the franchise grid is one less brick in your own fortress. True sovereignty is won or lost in these invisible, daily margins. If you want to break out of the robot matrix once and for all, you must stop chasing the big, loud numbers—and start guarding the small ones.

EPILOGUE: THE TWO BROTHERS (THE DUAL AUDIT OF TIME)

Two brothers stand on the same Mediterranean shore. They share the same Porcelain DNA, the same 1915 history of survival, and the same parents. They grew up in the same fortress in Beirut, eating the same bread and dreaming under the same stars. One is not "better" than the other—they are simply operating on different Frequencies. Levon, the Brother of the Clog, chose the path of Stability. He became the "Receiver" because that is what the "Academic Fog" promised would protect the family. He stayed in the system, wore the "Institutional Suit", and followed the rules with a heart of gold. His loyalty is his strength. He was the Shield that stayed behind to protect the tradition, while I became the Bayonet that moved forward to annex the future.

THE TRAGEDY OF THE MAP

My brother is a man of honor. He has been the "Stone" in my life when my own "Glitches" turned into fires. But the tragedy of his path is not his character—it is the Map he was given. He followed the "Printed Lie" because he believed it was the only way to be "Safe". He traded 40 years of his life

(14,600 days) for the 30-Day Punishment because he wanted to provide. He is a "High-Earning Robot" not by choice, but by Programming. When I look at him, I don't see a "Loser"; I see a General of Loyalty who was trapped in a Digestive System that doesn't care about his heart.

THE 1-DEGREE DIVERGENCE

At age 25, the gap between us was invisible. But the divergence began with a single degree of intent. The Clog Path: Seeking status, corporate validation, and the "Gilded Cage" of Pasadena. The Stone Path: Seeking weightlessness, the Cane Gold of our grandfather, and the silence of Sanary. Forty years later, the divergence is total. One is still listening for the bell of the "Hamster Wheel." The other is a Sovereign Ghost in a linen shirt, where the "Milk" is bottled and the silence is absolute.

THE EMPIRICAL VERDICT

(THE 28.7% STRIKE)

He stayed in the system, wore the Institutional Suit, and followed the rules with a heart of gold.

In the "Social Mirage", a 5% return is considered "Success." To the Sovereign Merchant, 5% is a "Clog."

We do not play for crumbs; we play for Weightlessness.

Here is the mathematical proof of the 3 P.I.G.s:

1. THE DEPLOYMENT (The Seed)

Initial Acquisition (P.I.G.s 1 & 2): $164,000

Second Acquisition

(P.I.G. 3): $83,000

Strategic Renovations: $73,000

TOTAL CAPITAL AT RISK: $320,000

2. THE HARVEST (The Milk)

P.I.G. 1 (X1 Miles): $36,000/year

P.I.G. 2 (X2 Miles): $21,600/year

P.I.G. 3 (X3 Miles): $34,320/year

TOTAL ANNUAL MILK: $91,920

3. THE SOVEREIGN RATIO

$91,920 (Annual Milk) ÷ $320,000 (Total Capital at Risk) = 28.7% Annual Cash-on-Cash Return

The Velocity: At this rate, you recapitalize your entire investment every 3.5 years. This yield is produced with 0-Debt. No bank. No interest. No "Vultures".

THE INHERITANCE AUDIT

When the Brother of the Clog finishes his path, he leaves behind a "Full House" of logistical complexity. He leaves an estate of static remnants—the "Primary Debris" of contracts, obligations, and administrative ties that have lost their velocity. His heirs inherit the labor of sorting through a stationary life. In contrast, the heirs of the Stone inherit an Artery. They do not have to "sort" or resolve the past—the yield simply arrives in their accounts while they sit in the Mediterranean sun. They inherit Time.

THE PROPELLER OF GOODNESS

The ultimate difference is in the "Why." The Brother of the Clog is stationary. Even at 71, he is looking for a way to extract value from a system that is already finished with him. The Brother of the Stone is a Propeller. Because his survival is decoupled from his effort, he is free to be a Sovereign Guest of the World. He uses the "Monthly Honey" to fund the "Makers" and give the world the Frequency of Truth.

NOT TO DECIDE IS TO DECIDE

By refusing to unlearn the "Printed Lie," you have decided to remain a slave to the 30-Day Trap. My brother didn't "choose" the Clog; he simply decided not to leave it. If you do not build your Artery while you have the strength, you are deciding to be a Sovereign Beggar in your winter years.

THE EXIT STRIKE:

THE BIRTH OF THE 4TH P.I.G.

As the ledger for The Orazon Protocol closes, a new Artery begins to pulse. To the "Robot," this is merely a book. To you, the "Maker," this is the 4th P.I.G.— the first Digital Stone in the Orazon fortress. This is your gateway to Infinite Change, and here is the breakdown of the strike: The Digital Stone (Asymmetric Weightlessness): The first 3 P.I.G.s are anchored in the heat of the California desert; they are heavy, physical, and stationary. The 4th P.I.G. is the first asset with Zero Biological Overhead. There is no "Bath" to perform here. There are no property taxes, no leaking pipes, and no mortgages. It is pure, weightless yield. The $50M Verdict (The Master Markup): The 4th P.I.G .was not born from a desire for "Status", but from the silence of the Vultures. When the "Blind Icari" of the corporate world were offered the chance to annex this wisdom for $10 million each, they chose the "Social Clog" over

Sovereignty. Their silence was the greatest Intrinsic Gift. It allowed for a fresh revaluation. What you are holding was once a "Deal"; it is now a Sovereign Movement. The Gateway to the Zenith: This asset marks the definitive transition from Extraction (Phase III) to the Zenith (Phase V). By holding this truth, you are witnessing the moment the General officially exited the "Receiver" mindset. The 4th P.I.G. is the ultimate tool for the Sovereign Ghost. While the General sits in the peace of Sanary-sur-Mer, practicing the art of "Doing by Doing Nothing," this digital Artery pumps "Monthly Honey" globally —untouchable, unceasing, and invisible to the Vultures.

A NOTE TO MY BROTHER, LEVON

I recognize the iron discipline you have demonstrated in mastering the legacy our father entrusted to you—the relentless focus of the jewelry trade and the heavy weight of leadership. You are a soldier of the "Hard Way," a master of the tangible world who chose the path of duty to guard the family Octagon. If I have contrasted our paths in this manual, it is to show that your strength provided the baseline from which I could explore the Artery. It is not a critique of your life, but a testament to the weight you carried so that those you love could move with freedom. You guarded the physical treasures so that I could find the philosophical Stone. We are two sides of the same Armenian coin, honorably carrying the Der Boghossian heritage and legacy; you provided the necessary stability, and I chose to flip mine into the sun of Sanary, so the light would reach Berj and Janine.

THE SOVEREIGN GHOST

(THE FINAL SIGNATURE)

I sit here in Sanary-sur-Mer, watching the light fade over the harbor. It is the same Sun that watched the fire in 1915. I am the Brother of the Stone. I have outsmarted the borders, the banks, and my own vanity. The Orazon Protocol is now yours. You have the Keys. You have the Algorithm. You have the Absolute Truth. 💎

The Bell has rung. The hammer is in your hand.
STRIKE IT !!

VASKEN DER BOGHOSSIAN

Sanary-Sur-Mer, France — May 2026

APPENDIX: THE ANCESTRAL CABLE—A LETTER TO THE NEXT GENERATION

To Berj, Aren, Garine, Janine, Lori, and the Young Vaskens who follow:

You are reading these words because you have inherited a Map, not a "Fortune". A fortune can be siphoned by "Vultures" or evaporated by the "Social Clog", but a Map is an Absolute Truth that lives inside your own skin.

I write this from the Sanary Zenith, watching the tide reflect the same sun that saw our bloodline nearly extinguished in 1915. Our grandfather Levon did not survive the "Hard Way" so that you could become "Academic Robots" or "Receivers" of a 30-day punishment. He survived so that you could become Makers.

Here are your specific coordinates for holding the perimeter:

To Berj & Aren:

You carry the names and the heavy legacy of the men who forged our stone. Your primary command is to guard the physical fortress, keep the arteries debt-free, and ensure the milk of the desert continues to bottle itself in total silence. Never let a corporate clerk or an academic map complicate the clean architecture I have handed you. But heed this warning with extreme vigilance: your most lethal threat will never come from an obvious enemy, because those are easy to spot and bypass. Your true danger lies in the unpredictable enemy disguised as a friend. Watch the people closest to you. The "friends" who smile at your table while harboring silent, toxic envy are the ones who will try to siphon your light because they cannot bear to see you conquer the heights. Guard your perimeter ruthlessly, and never let counterfeit loyalty breach the walls of your sanctuary.

To Garine:

You possess the sharp sensors to spot the glitches in a world blinded by social fog. Your command is to maintain absolute financial and metabolic hygiene. Look at the daily margins, protect the seed capital, and never trade your sovereign autonomy for a shiny mirage.

To Janine & Lori:

You are the carriers of the unyielding Porcelain DNA into the next era. Your command is to stay mobile, liquid, and invisible to the sensors of the system. Rent your sanctuary, own your pipe, and use the spillage of the artery to remain entirely weightless guests of the world.

THE SANARY ZENITH IS YOUR BIRTHRIGHT:

Seek the coordinates where the "Social Clog" is thinnest and the "Organic Truth" is loudest. Do not stop until you have achieved Absolute Zero; the state where you owe nothing to the "Vultures" and everything to the Architect.

THE 4th P.I.G. : THE INFINITE ARTERY:

Most will stop at the 3rd P.I.G. , believing the fortress is complete. But the 4th P.I.G. is the ultimate weapon. It is the transition from owning the "Metal" to owning the Message. By turning my life into this manual, I have built an Artery that does not rely on a physical location. A physical asset can be occupied, but a Sovereign Idea is a Ghost that cannot be caged. Use your 3 P.I.G.s to fund your freedom, but use your 4th P.I.G. to ensure that freedom is infinite. I have flipped my coin into the Sun so that the light reaches you.

The Orazon Protocol is now yours. You are no longer "Receivers" of the past; you are the Donors of the Future.

The Bell has rung. Build the Artery.

With the unyielding strength of the Forge,

Vasken Der Boghossian

A NOTE ON STRUCTURAL AUTHENTICITY

The Author is a Sovereign and an Architect of the Behavior Matrix, not a clerk of the academy. While this ledger has been forged under blue skies and blue-chip isolation, it has intentionally not been softened by the "Academic Polishing" of the Social Clog.

If you catch a typo or a repetition, congratulations: it simply means your neurological sensors are functioning and you are actually paying attention to the ledger. to the ledger .

Do not act like a blind heir staring at the wrong details. Focus on the math; ignore the slag.

Made in the USA
Monee, IL
04 November 2026

67387531R00177